IBC対訳ライブラリー

英語で読む 羽生結弦
The Yuzuru Hanyu Story

土屋晴仁 著
佐藤和枝 英訳
出水田隆文 英語解説

JN250717

カバー写真 ＝ Kyodo News / Getty Images
ナレーション ＝ Peter von Gomm
録音スタジオ ＝ 株式会社巧芸創作

はじめに

　2006年頃から現在にいたる10余年の間、日本はフィギュアスケートの世界でトップクラスの選手を輩出してきた。たとえば2006年のトリノ冬季五輪では女子シングルで荒川静香が金メダルを獲得。翌年に東京で開催された世界選手権では、安藤美姫、浅田真央がワン・ツー・フィニッシュ。浅田は2010年バンクーバー五輪でも銀メダルだった。男子は2007年世界選手権で高橋大輔が銀メダルとなり、2010年のバンクーバー冬季五輪でも銅メダルを獲得した。この流れを決定づけ、世界中が「フィギュア大国・ニッポン」に注目するようになったのは、ひとりの若者の大活躍がある。

　若者の名は羽生結弦。2012年の世界選手権で3位に入賞したのを皮切りに、2014年ソチ五輪で優勝。2014年2017年世界選手権も制し、GP（グランプリ）ファイナルは2013年から16年まで4連覇（2013年–2016年）。また、SP（ショートプログラム）と、FS（フリースケーティング）の総合得点で世界最高記録を次々と更新して今も記録保持者であり、2013年10月より世界ランキング1位を保持している。

　1994年に仙台市に生まれ、4歳の時、姉と一緒に地元のリンクに通うになったのがスケートとの出会いだった。ジャンプやスピンが大好きですぐに才能を発揮して注目を集めた。同郷の荒川静香やロシアの選手で「帝王」と呼ばれたプルシェンコに憧れ、自分も世界の大舞台で活躍したいと猛練習を重ねた。しかし2011

年3月東北地方を襲った大地震と津波の被害者になった。この被災にもめげずに翌年ニースでの世界選手権に最年少で出場し、3位に入賞。……いや、これ以上のストーリーは、本文を読んでもらうことにしよう。

　羽生は、独特である。まず際立っているのが、その容姿や卓越したスケーティング技術が生み出す華麗さと力強さ。それを支えているのが負けず嫌いで強気の性格だが、試合のたびに自分の演技を振り返り、そこから修正すべきことを把握していく冷静な頭脳も持ち合わせている。さらに、自分を支えてくれるコーチやスタッフ、家族などへの感謝の気持ちを持ち続けていることも、彼らしさといえる。リンクへの出入りの時には必ず一礼し、メダルをもらえば、母の首にかけるのが彼の習慣だ。これらのすべてが羽生ファンを急増させてきた。

　しかし、本書を書きあげた時、ファンたちを不安にさせる事故が起きた。2017-2018シーズンつまり韓国・平昌での冬季五輪に向けた戦いが始まっていた11月、プログラムに加えようとして高難度の「4回転ルッツ」を練習中に転倒。右足関節の靱帯を損傷し、GPシリーズへの参加を見送ったのだ。五輪まで残りわずか3ヵ月……。彼の一日も早い復帰を願うしかない。それにしても、彼の本当の長い人生ストーリーは、まだ始まったばかり。本書の読者とともにその目撃者、証言者になれることはラッキーだと思う。

2017年　12月8日の羽生の23歳の誕生日を前にして

土屋　晴仁

本書の構成

本書は、

- □ 英日対訳による本文　　□ 欄外の語注
- □ 覚えておきたい英語表現　□ MP3形式の英文音声

で構成されています。

　本書は、フィギュアスケーター羽生結弦の物語を英語／日本語で読み進めながら、同時に役立つ英語表現も学んでいけるように構成されています。

　各ページの下部には、英語を読み進める上で助けとなるよう単語・熟語の意味が掲載されています。また英日の段落のはじまりが対応していますので、日本語を読んで英語を確認するという読み方もスムーズにできるようになっています。またストーリーの途中に英語解説がありますので、本文を楽しみながら、英語の使い方などをチェックしていただくのに最適です。

付属のCD-ROMについて

本書に付属のCD-ROMに収録されている音声は、パソコンや携帯音楽プレーヤーなどで再生することができるMP3ファイル形式です。一般的な音楽CDプレーヤーでは再生できませんので、ご注意ください。

■音声ファイルについて

　付属のCD-ROMには、本書の英語パートの朗読音声が収録されています。本文左ページに出てくるヘッドホンマーク内の数字とファイル名の数字がそれぞれ対応しています。

　パソコンや携帯プレーヤーで、お好きな箇所を繰り返し聴いていただくことで、発音のチェックだけでなく、英語で物語を理解する力が自然に身に付きます。

■音声ファイルの利用方法について

　CD-ROMをパソコンのCD/DVDドライブに入れて、iTunesなどの音楽再生(管理)ソフトにCD-ROM上の音声ファイルを取り込んでご利用ください。

■パソコンの音楽再生ソフトへの取り込みについて

　パソコンにMP3形式の音声ファイルを再生できるアプリケーションがインストールされていることをご確認ください。

　CD-ROMをパソコンのCD/DVDドライブに入れても、多くの場合音楽再生ソフトは自動的に起動しません。ご自分でアプリケーションを直接起動して、「ファイル」メニューから「ライブラリに追加」したり、再生ソフトのウインドウ上にファイルをマウスでドラッグ&ドロップするなどして取り込んでください。

　音楽再生ソフトの詳しい操作方法や、携帯音楽プレーヤーへのファイルの転送方法については、ソフトやプレーヤーに付属のマニュアルで確認するか、アプリケーションの開発元にお問い合わせください。

目次

Part 1

A genius boy in Sendai!

天才少年が仙台にいる！

[01] At the age of four, joins a skating class with his sister

Yuzuru Hanyu was born on December 7, 1994 in Sendai, Miyagi Prefecture. His father is a junior high school teacher and his mother works in the menswear section of a local supermarket. He has a sister who is four years older than him.

Yuzuru has had asthma since he was two. But when he learned that Hiroyasu Shimizu, a gold medalist in speed skating at the Nagano Olympics, also had the same disease, he started to think about learning skating as well. He began skating in the spring of 1998 when he was four years old, together with his sister. They used to walk to the Izumi Daiei Olympic Sports Club, a local skating rink at a nearby shopping mall. Minoru Sano, a famous former figure skater, was teaching skating for children there.

This skating rink was the only one in the Tohoku region open 24 hours all year round. It was the home turf of Shizuka Arakawa, a gold medalist at the Torino Olympics in 2006, so it is also known as the "Arakawa Rink."

■menswear 图 紳士服　■asthma 图 喘息　■as well 同じように　■used to do よく～していた　■all year round 一年中　■home turf 本拠地

4歳、姉と一緒に「スケート教室」に通う

　羽生結弦は、1994年12月7日、宮城県仙台市北西部にあるベッドタウン泉区で生まれた。中学校教員の父と、地元スーパーの紳士服売り場で働く母、4つ年上の姉という4人家族。

　結弦は、2歳の時、小児喘息を発症したが、長野五輪スピードスケートの金メダリストである清水宏保が、同じ病気を持ちながらも活躍したことを知って、自分もスケートを習いたいと思うようになった。彼がスケートを始めたのは、1998年4歳の春。地元のスケートリンク「泉DOSCアイスアリーナ」に、姉と一緒に通うようになってからだ。スーパーマーケットであるダイエーのショッピング・モール付属施設であり、歩いて通えた。ここで、元フィギュアスケート選手として活躍した佐野稔の「子どもスケート教室」が開催されていた。

　このスケートリンクは、東北地方唯一の24時間、通年滑走可能なリンクであり、日本人女子フィギュアで初めてトリノ五輪（2006年）金メダリストになった荒川静香のホームグラウンドでもあったために「荒川リンク」とも呼ばれる。

When children begin figure skating, they learn fundamental skating techniques at the start, such as how to use the edges of their skates, shift their body and do simple turns. And they gradually become fascinated with "collecting badges." They can get badges after they have passed skating skills tests. There are eight skill levels. Only the children who have reached the third level or above can participate in official competitions.

If you are nine or 10 years old, or a third or fourth grader, and if you have passed Level 3 of the badge test, you can enter "Novice B" class tournaments. If you are one to two years older than that and have passed Level 4 or above, you can enter "Novice A" tournaments.

However, passing Level 3 is not that easy. You have to pass all three categories of the test: elements, steps and free. The elements part tests one's grasp of the fundamental techniques, but it includes a lot of different things: the "axel jump" (to jump up off one foot, turn around one and a half times in the air and land on the other foot on the ice), the "double jump," the "camel spin with more than five rotations" (a spin with the leg and the upper body in a horizontal line), the "spin combination" and the "flying spin" (a spin after a jump). And all these have to be performed within two minutes.

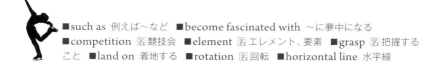

■such as 例えば〜など ■become fascinated with 〜に夢中になる
■competition 图競技会 ■element 图エレメント、要素 ■grasp 图把握する
こと ■land on 着地する ■rotation 图回転 ■horizontal line 水平線

フィギュアスケートを始めた子供たちは、まず基本的なスケーティング技術を学ぶ。エッジの使い方、体重の移動の仕方、簡単なターン。そして次第に「バッジ集め」に夢中になる。バッジというのは、スケート技術の上達度に応じたテストを受けてもらえる等級別のバッジである。初級から８級まである。３級以上にならないと正式な競技大会には出られない。

　年齢にして９〜10歳、学年なら小学校３〜４年で、バッジテスト３級に合格していれば、「ノービスＢ」というクラスの大会に出ることができる。その上の１〜２歳年長で４級以上になると「ノービスＡ」になる。「ノービス」は、「初心者・新米」の意味だ。

　３級といっても、決して簡単ではない。エレメンツ、ステップ、フリーという３種目すべてに合格しなくてはならない。基本技術を見るエレメンツだけでも、「アクセルジャンプ」（片足で踏み切ってジャンプし、一回半回転して他方の足で着地する）、「ダブルジャンプ」、「５回転以上のキャメル・スピン」（挙げた片足と上体が水平一直線の姿勢のまま行うスピン）、「スピン・コンビネーション」、「フライング・スピン」（跳び上がってからのスピン）などを２分間の間に演じなくてはならない。

Young Yuzuru started to love spins and jumps. When Yuzuru was six, Daisuke Takahashi, who was eight years his senior, was practicing at the same rink. This was stimulating for Yuzuru. And under Shoichiro Tsuzuki's instruction, his skating techniques improved very quickly. But he preferred playing with his friends rather than practicing skating. His father was a baseball coach at his junior high school. "I wanted to play baseball rather than skate," said Yuzuru later. His parents told him, "You can stop practicing figure skating if you like. It would be helpful for us because we wouldn't have to spend so much money." But he did not stop skating.

"I didn't want to quit. The reason I started skating was because I was fascinated by skaters. I practiced so hard. And I liked to wear costumes made by my mother, and to perform in front of an audience," he said.

Around that time, he planned his own program for the first time. His inspiration for the choreography was "Ultraman Gaia," his favorite hero on TV. The next one was Foster's "Camptown Races."

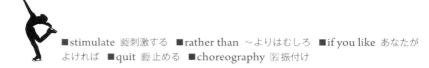

■stimulate 動刺激する　■rather than ～よりはむしろ　■if you like あなたが
よければ　■quit 動止める　■choreography 图振付け

幼い結弦は、スピンやジャンプが大好きになった。6歳の頃、8歳上（中学2年、14歳）の「お兄さん」高橋大輔が同じリンクに練習に来ていたことも刺激になった。都築章一郎の指導を受けて、結弦のスケート技術は、みるみるうちに上手くなっていった。しかし、本人は友達と遊びたい盛りだから、ハードな練習は好きではなかったようだ。父が中学校で野球部の監督をしていたこともあり、「本当は野球がしたかった」と後に語っている。両親は「止めてもいいよ。お金がかからなくて助かる」と言った。でもスケートは止めなかった。

　「選手たちに憧れて始めたことだから止めたくなかった。せっかくここまで頑張ってきたのだから。それに母が作ってくれるコスチュームを着て、お客さんが注目してくれる中で演技するのは好きだった」

　その頃、自分のプログラムを初めて考えた。振付けのイメージは、大好きだった『ウルトラマン・ガイア』。次に選んだのは、フォスターの『草競馬』だった。

A genius mushroom haircut boy

In 1994, the year Yuzuru was born, the Olympic Winter Games were held in Lillehammer, Norway (1994), then in Nagano, Japan (1998), Salt Lake City, United States (2002), Turin, Italy (2006), Vancouver, Canada (2010) and Sochi, Russia (2014). In 2018, the Games will be held in PyeongChang, South Korea. The medalists in each of these Games have become heroes and heroines for young skaters. Yuzuru was fascinated by Evgeni Plushenko of Russia.

Plushenko was born in November, 1982. Like Yuzuru, he had a weak constitution, and he learned Russian dance and figure skating to improve his constitution. He became famous after his first win at the World Championships when he was 18. He won a silver medal in Salt Lake City when he was 20, gold in Turin and silver in Vancouver. He is a three-time World Champion, a seven-time European Champion, a four-time Grand Prix Final Champion and a 10-time consecutive Russian Champion. He won the Cup of Russia eight consecutive times, a record-breaking achievement. He is 173 centimeters (five feet 10 inches) tall. His nickname is the "Emperor," and his trademark is his blond mushroom haircut.

■be held in ～て開催される ■constitution 图体質 ■win a medal メダルを獲得する ■consecutive 厖連続の

「マッシュルーム・カットの天才少年」

　結弦が生まれた1994年以降の冬季五輪は、ノルウェー・リレハンメル（94年）、日本・長野（98年）、米・ソルトレイクシティ（02年）、イタリア・トリノ（06年）、カナダ・バンクーバー（10年）、ロシア・ソチ（14年）と開催され、2018年は韓国・平昌と続く。その度ごとに活躍したメダリストたちが幼いスケーターたちが憧れるヒーローやヒロインになった。結弦が夢中になったのは、ロシアのエフゲニー・プルシェンコだった。

　プルシェンコは、1982年11月生まれ。彼もまた、幼い時は虚弱で、それを克服するためにロシアン・ダンスとフィギュアスケートを習ったという経歴を持つ。18歳で世界選手権に初優勝して知られるようになり、20歳のソルトレイクシティで銀、トリノで金、バンクーバーで銀メダルを獲得。世界選手権優勝3回、欧州選手権優勝7回、GP（グランプリシリーズ）ファイナル優勝4回。ロシア選手権では出場した大会10回連続優勝。GPシリーズロシア杯8連続優勝という大記録を達成している。身長173cm、「皇帝」の異名を持ち、金色の長髪をマッシュルーム・カットにしているのがトレードマークだ。

Yuzuru changed his hairstyle to a mushroom haircut like Plushenko, his hero. He stood out at his home rink as he could execute excellent spins and jumps with his very slender body. In October 2004, when Yuzuru was nine, he participated in the eighth National Novice B Championships at the Meiji Jingu Gaien Ice Skating Rink. Although it was the first time he had participated in a Novice B competition, he won. In December 2004, he went on his first tour abroad. He won the Tampere Santa Claus Cup in Finland. For his freestyle routine, he performed to the movie theme tune, "From Russia with Love." On the podium, he raised the trophy up high like Plushenko always did. But when he smiled, it was noticeable that his front tooth was missing because his baby tooth had fallen out. At the end of that year, his home rink was closed down due to financial difficulties, and he had to practice at a rink that was quite far away from his home. This meant that he could not practice enough. As a result, he finished second at the National Novice B the following year, which he regretted for a long time after.

In 2006 when Yuzuru was 11, Shizuka Arakawa won the first gold medal for Japan in a dramatic turnabout at the Olympics in Turin. Also, Fumie Suguri succeeded in finishing an impressive fourth. In the previous year, Mao Asada won at the Grand Prix Final. But she could not participate in the Turin Olympics due

■stand out 目立つ　■execute 動 演じる、実行する　■participate 動 参加する
■podium 名 表彰台　■noticeable 形 目に付く　■fall out 抜ける　■close
down 閉鎖する　■due to 〜が原因で　■following 形 次の　■turnabout 名
逆転　■succeed 動 成功する

結弦はあこがれのプルシェンコを真似て、自分もマッシュルーム・カットにした。細いやせぎすの体型で、スピンやジャンプに抜群の切れ味を見せるこの少年は、名称が「コナミスポーツクラブ泉・スケートリンク」（KSC泉）となったリンクの中でもひときわ目立つ存在だった。そして2004年10月、9歳の時、東京・明治神宮スケート場で開催された第8回全日本ノービスBに初参加で優勝する。同じ年の12月、初の海外遠征。フィンランドでの「ダンペレ・サンタクロース杯」でも優勝した。フリーでは『ロシアより愛をこめて』で演技した。表彰台ではトロフィーを高く掲げてポーズをとった。もちろん、プルシェンコの真似であるが、その笑顔は幼歯が抜けて前歯がなかった。また年末にはホームリンクが経営難で閉鎖となり、少し離れた場所にあるリンク等で練習を続けた。そのため思うように練習が行えず、翌年のノービスBで2位になったことを後々まで悔しがった。

　11歳の2006年、トリノオリンピックで荒川静香が日本人として初の金メダルを劇的な逆転で獲得。村主章枝も4位と大健闘。また浅田真央が、前年の世界GP（グランプリ）ファイナルで優勝しながら、年齢規定（1990年9月生まれ）で出場できなかったことも話題になって、国内にフィギュアスケート熱が盛り上がっ

to the age regulations (she was born in September, 1990 and was not old enough to participate in the Olympics). These successes attracted many people to figure skating in Japan, and Sendai, "the holy place of figure skating," was the focal point of this popularity.

Yuzuru became the center of attention because of his remarkable records. He became the focus of interest as the "genius mushroom haircut boy" among people related to the Japan Skating Federation and in media such as skating magazines. The local TV station in Sendai ran a feature about Yuzuru, who was a sixth grader then. "I want to follow in the steps of gold medal winner Plushenko. He rarely makes mistakes in his program, and his strong appeal to the audience is great. I will win a gold medal in Sochi for the first time as a Japanese male skater like Ms. Arakawa did for women in Turin," he said in the interview.

It is Yuzuru's style to put his main objective into words to motivate himself. Young Yuzuru was the same. However, when he made that comment, he was in a slump. So maybe nobody took this 11-year-old boy's words seriously.

Yuzuru's home rink was reopened in November when he was 12. He participated in the 2007–2008 Japan Junior Championships held in Sendai, his home town, which was his first time. Usually, only 13- to 18-year-olds can enter the junior level, but Yuzuru was an exception. He came third, behind Takahito Mura, who is

■focal point 中心　■relate to ～に関わる　■run a feature about ～を特集する　■follow in the steps of ～の例にならう　■objective 图目標　■take someone's words seriously（人の）言葉を真面目に受け取る　■exception 图 特例

た。"聖地"仙台はその熱気の中心だった。

　こんな熱気に、活躍が目ざましい少年・結弦が炙りだされた。スケート協会の関係者やスケート雑誌メディアの間で、「仙台にマッシュルーム・カットの天才少年がいる」と話題になった。地元仙台のTV局は、小学6年生の結弦を特集した。そのインタビューの中で、彼はこう答えている。

　「目標は、男子で金メダルを取ったプルシェンコ選手です。プログラムの中でほとんどミスをせず、観客にアピールしているところがすごいです。ボクも、ソチ五輪では荒川選手に続いて、日本人男子初の金メダルを目指します」

　大きな目標をあえて言葉にして、自分のモチベーションにする彼の流儀はもうこの頃から芽生えていた。ただ、この時期、少し不調でもあった11歳少年の言葉を本気で聴いた人は誰もいなかったかもしれない。

　ホームリンクが再開された12歳の11月、結弦は、地元・仙台で開催された「2007-2008全日本ジュニア選手権」に初出場。ふつうジュニアのクラスは中高生、つまり13歳から18歳が出場するのだから、結弦は特例である。3つ年上の無良崇人、佐々木彰生に続いて3位に入賞した。小学生が「お兄さん」たちと戦って

three years older than him, and Akio Sasaki. It was the first time in Japan that an elementary school student had shared the podium with his "big brothers." But Yuzuru was not satisfied at all, and he did not hide his competitiveness.

"I want to win next year. I participate in games to win," he said.

Mastering the "triple axel" as a killer technique

Yuzuru entered a local junior high school in Sendai, and the junior class in skating. From 2005, Nanami Abe, who owns a local skate shop with her husband, was Yuzuru's coach and choreographer. Under her instruction, he mastered triple axels through hard training in the summer of 2008. He was 13.

The number of rotations in the air increases from a single to a double, and then to a triple that requires three rotations in the air. The four-rotation jump currently performed by top-class male skaters is called a quadruple. Technical points for jumps account for 40% of the overall points in the figure skating scoring system, and so it is a very important scoring element. There are six techniques (in ascending order of difficulty): the toe loop, Salchow, loop, flip, Lutz, and the axel—the most difficult one. Each technique will be explained later, but I will describe the axel

■not ~ at all まったく〜ない　■satisfy 動 満足する　■competitiveness 名 競争心　■killer 形 必殺の　■choreographer 名 振付師　■account for 〜の割合を占める　■ascending order 少ない順、昇順

表彰台に上ったのは日本初のこと。だから大健闘なのだが、結弦は満足しなかった。負けん気の強さを隠さなかった。

「来年は勝ちたい。せっかく試合に出るからには勝ちに行きたいです」

必殺技「トリプル・アクセル」をマスターする

　結弦は地元の仙台市立七北田中学校に進学してジュニアの仲間入りをした。2005年から、コーチと振付けは地元でスケートショップを夫婦で営む阿部奈々美が担当した。彼女の指導を受けながら、2008年、13歳（中２）の夏、猛特訓してトリプル・アクセルをマスターした。

　シングル、ダブルと空中での回転数が増え、トリプルは３回転する。なお、現在、男子のトップクラスが取り入れている４回転ジャンプは「クアドラプル」という。ジャンプはその技術点だけで、フィギュアスケートの採点全体の４割にも及ぶ、フィギュアスケートの重要な得点源であり、６種類の技がある。難しい順にあげると、「トゥ・ループ」「サルコウ」「ループ」「フリップ」「ルッツ」となり、最高難度が「アクセル」となる。個々の説明は後回しにして、「アクセル」だけ説明しておこう。これは19世紀末のノルウェー選手アクセル・パウルゼンが考案した。前進滑走

now. It was named after Axel Paulsen, a Norwegian athlete who was competing at the end of the 19th century. The skater starts by skating forward, jumps using the outside edge from one foot, rotates in the air, lands on the other foot, and glides backward. So it has an extra half rotation.

As of fall 2017, nobody has ever performed a quadruple axel. It is said that Yuzuru will be the first one to do so.

The triple axel that Yuzuru mastered in his junior high school years has become one of his strongest techniques. He demonstrated it for the first time at the 2008–2009 Japan Junior Championships in November where he had placed third in the previous year. He fell in two jumps and placed fourth in the short program (SP), but he performed the free skating (FS) cleanly to win the title overall. Only the winner of this competition qualifies for the World Junior Championships, which is approved by the International Skating Union (ISU). For the music, he used "Bolero" for the SP and "Rhapsody on a Theme of Paganini" for the FS. In December, he competed at the senior level in Nagano as the youngest skater ever, and surprisingly came eighth. But media attention was concentrated on Mao Asada, Miki Ando, Takahiko Kozuka, Nobunari Oda and others. "I will become Japan's second Olympic gold medalist," Yuzuru announced at the time. But this was not mentioned in any articles.

■compete 動競技に参加する　■glide 動滑る　■demonstrate 動披露する ■place third 3位になる　■qualify 動資格を得る　■be approved by 〜公認 の　■article 图 (新聞などの)記事

から片足のアウト・エッジで踏み切り，空中で回転、踏み切りと反対の足のアウト・エッジで後ろ向きに着氷し，そのまま後進滑走につなげる滑り方だ。向きが逆になる半回転分が多くなる。

2017年秋現在、「4回転アクセル」は誰も跳んだことがない。おそらく結弦が最初の人になるだろうと言われている。

それはともかく、この時期にマスターした「トリプル（3回転）・アクセル」は、その後、結弦が最も得意とする技の一つになる。そして初めて披露したのが、前年3位になった「2008-2009全日本ジュニア選手権」(11月)である。試合ではショート・プログラム（SP）で2つのジャンプを失敗して4位だったが、フリー・スタイル（FS）で巻き返して逆転で優勝した。優勝した1名だけが、国際スケート連盟（ISU）が公認する「世界ジュニア選手権」(JGP)への出場権を得られる試合だった。曲目は、SPが「ボレロ」、FSが「パガニーニの主題による狂詩曲」だった。驚くのは、翌12月に長野で行われた「大人」にも史上最年少で出場し8位に入る活躍を見せたことだ。しかしマスコミの取材は浅田真央や安藤美姫、小塚崇彦、織田信成などに集中。この時にも、「僕が日本で2人目の五輪金メダリストになります」と発言したのだが、記事にはならなかった。

From this season to the next, the 2009–2010 season, when Yuzuru was 13–15 years old, he grew quickly as a young skater. It was now 10 years since he had started skating at the age of four. At this point, he changed his SP music to "Mission: Impossible II." And in 2009, he had his first win at the Junior Grand Prix Torun Cup (GAM Nestlé Nesquik Cup) in Poland in September, placed first at the Croatia Cup in October, became the winner at the Japan Junior Championships for two years in a row in November, and finished first at the JGP Final as the youngest skater ever (14 years old) in December. Although he finished in sixth place at the Japan Championships in the same month, at the World Junior Championships in March, 2010, he performed the FS almost faultlessly to win at the age of 15. He was the fourth Japanese male skater to win, and the first ever Japanese male junior high school student to do so. At that time, his haircut was still in the mushroom style.

Yuzuru's last words as a 14-year-old:
"More than 99% of the people in the world don't know me. I want to increase the number of people who can recognize me by even 1% by doing my best. I'd like to perform well so that anybody who sees me will never forget my performance."

"I want to become a legend! I want to show the world something that only I was able to do for the first time in human history. I want my name to be remembered throughout history!"

■in a row 連続して　■ever 副これまでに　■finish in -th place 〜位に終わる ■faultlessly 副完璧に　■recognize 動〜をすでに知っている　■would like to 〜したい　■so that 〜となるように

このシーズンから次の2009−2010シーズンは、13 〜 15歳という若い結弦が急速な成長を見せた時期でもある。4歳からのスケート人生10年目だ。SP曲を「ミッション：インポッシブル2」にして臨み、2009年9月ポーランドのJGPトルン杯（ネスレ杯）で初優勝すると、10月クロアチア杯で優勝、11月全日本ジュニア選手権で2連覇、12月JGPファイナルで史上最年少（14歳）優勝、同月の全日本選手権は6位だったものの、15歳になった翌年3月世界ジュニア選手権、FSはほぼノーミスで優勝。これは日本男子では4人目、中学生での優勝は日本男子史上初だった。なお、マッシュルーム・カットはまだ健在だった。

　14歳最後の言葉。
　「まだまだ僕のことを知らない人が世の中に99％以上いるので、1％でも増えるように頑張っていきたいです。そして世の中の人全員が忘れられないような演技をしたい」

　「僕はレジェンドになりたい！　人類初の何かで、僕だけってことをみんなに見せたいな。羽生結弦の名前を歴史に刻みたいんだ！」

Growing up to become a true rival to the adults (senior-level skaters)

There were many talented Japanese male figure skaters during the past 10 years, and the situation is the same now. At the top of the list are Daisuke Takahashi (born in 1986), Nobunari Oda (born in 1987) and Takahiko Kozuka (born in 1989), and they have always dominated the top of the championship rankings. Other strong skaters include Daisuke Murakami, Takahito Mura, Kento Nakamura (all three of whom were born in 1991), and Keiji Tanaka who was born in the same year as Yuzuru (1994). So Yuzuru was not the only one who was performing well during this period. Any one of them could have won at any championship, and this situation will be the same going forward. Young skaters are coming along fast, such as Shoma Uno, who is three years younger than Yuzuru, and Sota Yamamoto who was born in 2000.

To become the best in the face of such strong competition, gaining accolades such as "the youngest-ever winner" or "excellent for a junior level skater" are not good enough. Yuzuru had to grow to become a true rival to the adult skaters (seniors). To achieve that goal, in addition to his youthfulness and rashness, he needed thorough knowledge of the strengths and weaknesses of his rivals.

■dominate 動~を支配する　■include 動（主語の中に）~がいる　■go forward 進行する　■accolade 名 称賛の言葉　■in addition to ~に加えて　■rashness 名 ガムシャラさ

大人<ruby>たち<rt>シニア</rt></ruby>を本気で脅かす存在に成長

　今でもそうだが、ほぼ10年前から日本男子フィギュアの選手層は厚い。1986年生まれの高橋大輔を筆頭に織田信成（1987年生）や小塚崇彦（1989年生）が常に上位を占め、1991年生まれの村上大介、無良崇人、中村健人がおり、同年（1994年）生まれには田中刑事がいる。この時期、結弦ひとりが頑張っているわけではなかったし、誰が勝ってもおかしくない状況は今後も続く。3つ年下の宇野昌磨や2000年生まれの山本草太など若手の成長も著しい。

　そんな厳しい競争状態の中から抜きん出るには、「史上最年少」とか「ジュニアにしてはよく健闘している」と評価されるレベルでは通用しない。大人たちを本気で脅かす存在に成長しなくてはならない。若々しさやガムシャラさだけではなく、自分とライバルたちの強みと弱みを知り尽くし、したたかかつしな

In other words, he had to "fight like an adult" in order to be able to respond strongly and flexibly. To qualify for the senior level a skater has to be 15 years old or older and rank seventh or higher in the badge tests of the Japan Skating Federation. In the 2010–2011 season, this was the task that Yuzuru had to complete as he became a high school student who was now just over 170 centimeters (five feet seven inches) tall.

Let me explain the figure skating event "calendar." The figure skating annual calendar starts on July 1 and ends at the end of June the following year. To qualify for the Olympic Games, an athlete should be at least 16 years of age during that calendar year. That was why Mao Asada could not participate in the 2006 Turin Olympics because she was 15 years and 10 months old at that time. The local event season starts in the middle of summer in Japan, and the national competitions start around September. The athletes who win the national events proceed to the world events starting in November and December. In the Grand Prix Series of competitions, which are held in six countries (the United States, Canada, China, France, Russia and Japan), only the six skaters with the highest points in those six competitions qualify for the Grand Prix Final. After January, following the national championships series in each country, the European and Four Continents Championships are held, and finally the World

■in other words つまり ■let me explain 説明させてください ■calendar year 年度、暦年 ■proceed to 〜へ進む

やかに対応できる「大人の戦い方」が必要になる。シニアクラス
は、15才以上でシングル7級以上である。高校生になり身長も
170cmを超えた2010-2011シーズンの結弦の課題は、まさにこ
れだった。

　ここでスケート競技会の「カレンダー」の話をしておこう。ス
ケート界の1年は毎年7月1日に始まり、翌年の6月末に終わ
る。五輪出場資格はその年度内に16歳以上になっていなくては
ならない。だから15歳10ヵ月だった浅田真央は、2006年トリ
ノ五輪に出場できなかった。真夏に始まるシーズンは、国内各
地でのローカルな大会から始まり、9月頃から全日本クラスの戦
いになる。この試合に勝ちぬいて臨む国際大会は11月〜12月で
ある。世界6ヵ国（アメリカ、カナダ、中国、フランス、ロシア、
日本）が試合会場になるグランプリシリーズが始まり、6戦でポ
イントの高い順に上位6選手だけがグランプリファイナルに出
場できる。また、年が明けてから各国の国内選手権の後、ヨー
ロッパ選手権／四大陸選手権があり、3月の世界選手権（ワール
ド）でシーズンのピークを迎える。世界選手権で上位に入賞した
人は、翌シーズンのグランプリシリーズにシードされ、そのう
ちの2つに出られる。オリンピックの国別出場枠も前年のワー
ルドで決まる。

Championships takes place in March. The high-ranking athletes at the World Championships are named in the Grand Prix Series for the following year, and they can participate in two events in the series. The number of sports in the Olympics for each country is determined by the results of the World Championships in the previous year.

The strategy that Yuzuru focused on was "how to get high scores." To win at the senior level, he thought that doing "quadruple jumps" were absolutely necessary as everybody had started to do them now. First, he tried to master "quadruple toe loops." To execute this jump, the skater lifts up their left foot behind them, then jumps with an assist from the toe pick. Although this is one of the simplest jumps, rotating four times in the air is not very easy. Furthermore, near the end of a performance, the skater is exhausted and lacks in concentration.

Yuzuru was successful in executing quadruple toe loops at the GP Series (NHK Trophy in Japan) in October. But those jumps were not stable, and he placed fourth. At the following GP Cup in Russia, he finished seventh because he made minor mistakes in the consecutive jumps. According to the rules at that time, if a skater repeated the same kind of jumps, all those jumps were scored as zero. He lost as much as eight points due to this rule. (Under the current rules, only the repeated jumps are scored as

■take place 開催される　■spot 图（出場などの）枠　■strategy 图戦略　■focus on 〜に焦点をおく　■absolutely 副絶対に　■toe pick トゥピック《スケート靴の金属部分の先端》　■exhausted 形体力が尽きた　■stable 形安定した　■minor 形小さな　■according to 〜に従って

結弦が立てた戦略は、「いかにして高配点を獲得するか」だった。シニアの世界で戦って勝つには、誰もが跳ぶようになった「４回転ジャンプ」が欠かせないと考え、まずは「４回転トゥ・ループ」をマスターすることに取り組んだ。これは左足を大きく後ろに引き、トゥ（つま先）を付いて、その蹴る力で跳ぶ。一番簡単な部類のジャンプであるとはいえ、４回転だからそう簡単には決まらない。終盤には体力もなくなり集中力も続かない。

　10月のGPシリーズ（日本・NHK杯）では成功させたが安定せず４位。続くGPロシアでは７位。連続ジャンプのちょっとしたミスだった。「同じジャンプを繰り返したらそのジャンプすべてが０点になる」という当時のルールにより８点もの減点になったのだ（現在は、重複したジャンプだけ０点）。ミスしたらリカバリーするという作戦を考えられるほど成熟していなかった。だが、気を取り直した12月の全日本選手権で４位になり、四大陸

zero.) Yuzuru was not mature enough then to be able to implement an instant recovery strategy to mitigate his mistakes. But he pulled himself together and placed fourth in the Japan Championships in December, and was chosen to compete at the Four Continents Championships. In February 2011, at his first Four Continents Championships, he performed the quadruple toe loops successfully and won the silver medal. He was the youngest-ever skater to enter this competition (16 years old). Daisuke Takahashi, who "represents the high standard of the senior level", won the gold medal.

For Yuzuru, this season was one of trial and error. He challenged the seniors and realized once again that he lacked physical strength, but he was gradually gaining some confidence as well. And in Russia, he was fascinated by Patrick Chan (born in 1990) and thought of him as a new rival. The thought of competing against Chan at the 2014 Sochi Olympics in Russia gave him a renewed fighting spirit. He declared to reporters, "I will definitely come to the Sochi Olympics. And I will win!"

■mature 形 成熟した ■implement 動 実践する ■mitigate 動 軽減する ■pull oneself together 気を取り直す ■represent 動 ～に相当する ■trial and error 試行錯誤 ■compete against ～と競い合う ■definitely 副 絶対に

選手権に選出される。翌2011年2月、史上最年少（16歳）で初出場した台北での四大陸選手権では「4回転トゥ・ループ」を決めて銀メダル。優勝したのは"シニアの壁"として立ちはだかる高橋大輔だった。

　試行錯誤しながらのこのシーズン、シニアたちに挑戦し、体力不足を再認識したものの、少しずつ自信もついた。そしてロシアでは新たなライバルとして、カナダのパトリック・チャン（1990年生まれ）に釘付けになった。ロシアで開催される2014年のソチ五輪には彼と戦うのだと考えると、闘志がわいてきた。記者たちに向かって、「ソチ五輪には絶対に来ます。来て勝ちます！」と宣言した。

⟶Column 1⟵ Jumps in figure skating

A jump is a technique where the skater jumps and rotates in the air, which is a highlight in a performance. But if the speed just before the toe pick is not fast enough or the height of the jump is not high enough, the rotation becomes insufficient or the skater might fall on the ice on landing. So the jump becomes more difficult as the number of rotations increases. The entry to the jump varies and there are six kinds. Let me explain these in ascending order from the simplest to the most difficult. (Please note that the letters in parentheses are abbreviations for the techniques.)

1. Toe loop (T): While skating forward on the left foot outside edge, the skater turns backward, plants the left foot well behind the right foot, and picks the ice with the left toe and jumps.

2. Salchow (S): While skating forward on the left foot outside edge, the skater turns backward momentarily. Utilizing the rotational power, the jump is done with a swing of the right foot to forward-left. As this jump does not use the toe, it becomes more difficult than the toe loop as the number of rotations increases.

3. Loop (Lo): The skates on the ice draw loops. The skater draws an almost straight backward curve. The face does not look forward but almost looks down at the take off point. While skating backward on the right foot outside edge, the skater picks the toe of the same foot and lands on the same foot. At a glance it looks as if the skater has jumped with both feet together. Often, the loop is combined with other jumps in jump combinations.

〔コラム1〕 ジャンプの種類

　ジャンプは、跳び上がって空中で回転する技で、演技の華である。しかし、踏み切り直前のスピードや跳び上がる高さが十分でないと回転が不十分になったり、着氷時に転倒したりするので、回転数が増えるほど難しくなる。ジャンプへの入り方にも様々な形があり、6種類に分けられる。難易度の簡単な順に説明しよう（カッコの中は技の略称）。

　1. トゥ・ループ（T）：左足の前向きアウト・エッジで助走してきた後、後ろ向きに方向転換し、左足を後ろに下げ、左足のトゥ（つま先部分）をついてジャンプする。

　2. サルコウ（S）：左足の前向きアウト・エッジで滑ってきて、途中で後ろ向きにターン。その回転力を利用して、右足を左前方向に振り上げてジャンプする。トゥを使わないので、回転数が多くなるほど「トゥ・ループ」より難易度が高くなる。

　3. ループ（Lo）：足の軌跡がループ（輪）を描く。まっすぐに近い後ろ向きのカーブを描き、顔は前向きでなく、踏み切り地点をみるような感じになり、右足の後ろ向きアウト・エッジで踏み切り着氷も同じ足。一見、両足を揃えた姿勢でジャンプするように見える。ジャンプ・コンビネーションで、他のジャンプと組み合わされることが多い。

4. Flip (F): The skater glides forward and turns backward on the inside edge facing left. With the lowered right foot toe, the skater then jumps using both feet. As the toe pick edge is exactly the same as in the Salchow, it is known as the "toe Salchow" as well. But as the right foot is lowered and the body faces the opposite direction from the rotation direction, the number of rotations can be increased a little more than in the Salchow.

5. Lutz (Lz): The skater glides backward with the left foot outer edge, and, at the moment of the jump, takes off from the ice from the toe of the right foot. Up to this point, the skater draws a curve in a clockwise rotation, but at the time of the jump, the body rotates in the opposite direction. The Lutz is a counter-rotated jump. So the level of difficulty is higher than that of the other jumps even when the number of rotations is the same as the other ones.

6. Axel (A): Only this jump starts from a forward takeoff. And all the jumps are landed with the skater gliding backward. The skater glides forward and takes off from the outside edge of one foot, lands on the back outside edge of the other foot, and then continues to glide backward. An axel jump has an extra half rotation (180 degrees). Nobody has ever achieved a quadruple axel jump (4A), yet.

4. フリップ（F）：前向きでの滑走からターンし、左後ろ向きのイン・エッジに乗り、右足を後ろに下げてトゥをついてそのまま両足で踏み切ってジャンプする。踏み切りのエッジはサルコウと全く同じなので「トゥ・サルコウ」とも呼ばれるが、右足を後ろに下げ、体の向きが回転方向と逆を向くため、実質的な回転数が少し多くなる。

5. ルッツ（Lz）：後ろ向きに左足のアウト・エッジで滑走し、ジャンプする瞬間、右足のトゥを氷面に付けて踏み切る。それまでは時計周りのカーブを描いてきたのに、体は逆（カウンター）の反時計周りの方向に回転する。助走の力に逆らった方向に回転するため、回転数は同じでも難易度が増す。

6. アクセル（A）：このジャンプだけは前向きに踏み切る。ジャンプの着氷は全て後ろ向き。前進滑走から片足のアウト・エッジで踏み切り、反対の足のアウト・エッジで後ろ向きに着氷しそのまま後進滑走につなげる。他のジャンプよりも0.5回転多く回る。4回転アクセル（4A）は、人類未踏領域。

覚えておきたい英語表現

However, passing Level 3 is not *that* easy. (p. 12, 下から10行目)
しかしながら、３級に合格するのはそう簡単なことではない。

　英語を学び始めた人がほぼ必ず初期に学ぶ単語がthatでしょう。指示形容詞、指示代名詞としてはもちろん、関係代名詞や同格など様々な使い方がありますが、あまり学校で習わない使い方が副詞thatの使い方です。日常生活はもちろん、各種英語検定でも最近はよく出てきますので是非覚えておきましょう。

　　　　I can't run *that* fast.
　　　　私はそんなに速く走れません。

　　　　It's not *that* cheap.
　　　　それはそんなに安くないよ。

　これらのthatは形容詞や副詞の前に置かれて「そんなに」「それほど」という意味を表します。他の単語で置き換えるとsoに近いニュアンスを持っています。実は同様の使い方でthisもあります。

　　　　Who gave you *this* much money?
　　　　誰がこんなに君にお金をくれたんだい？

　thatが過去のことを指すのに対して、thisは現在のことを指します。thatが「遠い」イメージを持っていることを思い出せば理解しやすいですね。ちなみにsoは時間的に中立です。

It is Yuzuru's style to put his main objective into words to motivate himself. (p. 20, 下から9行目)
大きな目標を言葉にかえて、自分自身のやる気を引き出すのは結弦の流儀である。

It is A to B（Bは動詞）で「Bすることは A だ」という意味です。put はいろいろな言い方・使い方がある単語ですが、元々の意味は「～を置く」ですから、put A into B で「A を B に入れ込む」という直訳から、put A into words で「A を言葉にする」という意味になります。

I can't put my feeling into words.
この気持ちをどう表現していいか分からないよ。

Put this sentence into Japanese.
この文を日本語に訳しなさい。

他にも

To put it simply,...　　　簡単に言えば…

To put it another way,...　　別の言い方で言えば…

などの慣用的な表現もあります。
Motivate は「～の意欲を引き立てる」という意味の動詞です。羽生選手が強い精神力と強靭な体力、類い稀なテクニックを得ながら「絶対王者」と呼ばれるスケーターへ成長していく過程がこの言葉に表れています。読み進めるたび振り返っていただきたい言葉です。

Part 2

Affected by the Great East Japan Earthquake

3.11東日本大震災で被災

Spends four days at a shelter and loses home rink in Sendai

At 2:46:18 p.m. on Friday, March 11, 2011, a big earthquake with a magnitude of 9.0 occurred in the Tohoku region, and its epicenter was approximately 130 kilometers east-southeast of the Oshika Peninsula in Miyagi Prefecture. It was the biggest earthquake ever recorded in Japan. The Japanese government named this earthquake "The Great East Japan Earthquake." The earthquake triggered tsunami waves that reached heights of more than 10 meters, and coastal areas facing the Pacific Ocean in Tohoku and Kanto suffered a catastrophic disaster; 15,000 people were killed and more than 6,000 people were injured. The tsunami caused a meltdown in the reactors of the Fukushima Daiichi Nuclear Power Plant complex, causing a leakage of radioactive material that led to a huge nuclear incident.

At that time, Yuzuru was practicing at his home rink "Ice Rink Sendai" with his fellow senior skater Takumi Suenaga. The earthquake measured 6-upper around Sendai where the rink was located. As the area used to be paddy fields, the ground was not solid. As a result, the earthquake felt stronger than it really was.

■epicenter 图 震源地　■approximately 副 およそ　■trigger 動 ～を引き起こす　■catastrophic 形 壊滅的な　■nuclear power plant 原子力発電所　■complex 图 複合施設　■leakage 图 漏出　■fellow senior 同門の先輩　■measure 動 測定する　■paddy 图 水田　■solid 形 堅固な

４日間を避難所で暮らし、仙台のリンクも失う

　2011年3月11日（金曜日）午後2時46分18秒、宮城県牡鹿半島の東南東沖130kmを震源とするマグニチュード9.0の大地震が東北地方を襲った。日本周辺における観測史上最大の地震だった。政府はこの地震を「東日本大震災」と命名した。地震の結果、東北地方と関東地方の太平洋沿岸部に波高10m以上の津波が襲い、壊滅的な被害が発生した。死者は1万5千人、重軽傷者は6千人を超え、東京電力福島第一原子力発電所はメルトダウンして大量の放射性物質を漏洩。重大な原子力事故に発展した。

　その時、結弦は、ホームの「アイスリンク仙台」にいて、リンク内で、先輩の末永巧と一緒に練習中だった。リンクのある仙台市泉区周辺の震度は6強だったが、元は水田だった土地のため堅固な地盤ではない。体感的にはそれ以上の衝撃だった。

"I was so scared. The sound of shaking was really loud and beyond my imagination. I could hear the noise of the shelves of rental shoes shaking and the glass doors at the entrance breaking. All the doors were starting to open. I was crying and saying that this was impossible. I just hugged Takumi out of fear," said Yuzuru about the earthquake.

He had been traumatized by an earthquake before. When he was a third grader, he experienced the Miyagiken-oki earthquake in May, 2003. On that day in the evening, he was practicing at the same rink as well and felt five-upper quakes. He said about the Miyagiken-oki earthquake that he was afraid that his family might become separated.

Yuzuru escaped the rink with his skating shoes on. Usually, he put the covers on the edges of the skates for protection, but he didn't have time to do that then. Around the time of the quake, his sister was on her way home after her part-time job at the rink. His mother was at home and his father was out of the city on business. His sister was worried about Yuzuru and went back to the rink. After she had confirmed that he was all right, she went back home to take their mother to the rink, and finally they were able to be together.

■beyond 前〜の域を超えて　■out of fear 恐怖心から　■traumatize 動〜にトラウマを負わせる　■on one's way home 自宅に帰る途中で　■on business 仕事で　■confirm 動 確認する

「本当に怖かった。揺れている音が尋常じゃなくてこの世のものとは思えなかった。貸し靴の棚がガタガタと倒れる音、入り口のガラスのドアがはずれる音も聞こえ、そこらじゅうのドアがバーンって全部開いて行く。『いやいや、ちょっと待ってよ。無理でしょ、これ！』って、本気で泣いていました。『うわぁ、やだ！』って巧君にしがみついていました」

　結弦には地震へのトラウマがあった。小学校3年の2003年5月に起きた「宮城県沖地震」の思い出があったのだ。26日の夕方、やはりこのリンクでの練習中に震度5強の揺れに襲われ、家族がバラバラになってしまうのではないかという恐怖を感じたという。

　結弦はともかくスケート靴を履いたままリンクの外に避難した。氷上から上がる時はエッジにカバーを付けて保護するのだが、そんな余裕はなかった。その頃、姉はリンクでのアルバイト勤務を終えて自宅に帰る途中だった。母は自宅。父は仕事で市外にいた。弟を心配した姉はすぐにリンクへ戻り、結弦の安全を確認した後、自宅に帰って母と一緒にリンクに戻ってきた。家族3人はやっと合流できた。

But his house was partially destroyed and the bathroom was unusable. There was no electricity, gas or water. Nearby supermarkets were closed and people could not get food. Yuzuru's family was forced to spend four days at a nearby primary school gymnasium that had been converted into a shelter. The family finally learned the overall disastrous situation through the news on the radio. People were given only a small space and a blanket per person. Everybody was just barely surviving. But there was nothing to do at the shelter.

"I was thinking various things looking at the ceiling of the gymnasium," he remembers, like "It is not the right time for skating. It might be better for me to do volunteer work rather than skating…"

There was no clear plan for the restoration and reopening of the rink. Coach Abe was busy confirming the safety of all his students. Around that time, Yuzuru was able to contact Shoichiro Tsuzuki, his former coach, who had moved to the "Kanagawa Skate Rink" in Yokohama. He kindly agreed to accept Yuzuru at his rink for a short period of time only. Ten days after the disaster, Yuzuru moved to Yokohama with his damaged skating shoes. However, there were many members of this rink. And many of the skaters affected by the disaster in Tohoku and Kanto had gathered at this rink in search of a place to practice. This meant that he could

■electricity 图電気 ■be forced to 〜せざるを得ない ■gymnasium 图体育館 ■convert into 〜と化する ■shelter 图避難所 ■disastrous 形悲惨な ■ceiling 图天井 ■restoration 图復旧 ■This means that 〜ということである

しかし、実家の風呂にひびが入り半壊。電気・ガス・水道が使え ず、営業不能になったスーパーから食料を調達することもでき なくなった。結弦の一家は、避難所になった近くの小学校の 体育館で４日間過ごさざるを得なくなった。そこでラジオを通 して、初めて全体の被害状況を知ることになった。畳１帖分に 毛布１枚、誰もが、生きていくだけで精一杯の状況だった。避 難所では何もすることがない。

　「体育館の天井をぼんやり眺めながら、いろんなことを考えて いました。『もう、スケートなんかやっている場合じゃない』、 『ボランティアに行った方がいいのだろうか』など」

　リンクの復旧や再開のめどは立たず、阿部コーチも生徒たち の安否確認に追われていたが、その頃、横浜市の「神奈川スケー トリンク」に移っていたかつての先生、都築章一郎と連絡が取れ た。都築は、「短期間なら結弦を受け入れられる」と答えてくれ た。結弦は、被災から10日後、傷んだままのスケート靴を持っ て横浜に移動した。しかし、このリンクにはすでにたくさんの 会員がいたし、東北・関東圏で被災した多くのスケーターも練習 場所を求めて集まってきていた。朝と夕方に１時間ずつの練習 に参加するのがやっとだった。

practice only one hour in the morning and another hour in the evening.

Not long afterward, Yuzuru was offered the chance to participate in some ice shows during this off-season so that he could have some skating time. First, he would appear in an ice show held in support of the reconstruction on April 9 in Kobe.

"I was very thankful to know that there were many good people who helped me continue skating."

Ice shows are entertaining events held by various organizations. Athletes, including upper-ranked junior level and professional skaters from Japan and abroad, are invited. The shows are held in many places in Japan and are very entertaining events. There are often singers and live music performances, dance battles, clowns, acrobatics in the air and segments where skaters and fans can mingle. In that year, many ice show organizers got together to jointly hold an "ice show to promote recovery" about 60 times throughout Japan.

One of those ice shows was "THE ICE" held at the Niida Indoor Rink in Hachinohe City, Aomori on July 27. About 1,400 people who were living in temporary residences in three prefectures in Tohoku were invited to attend the show for free. A skating class for children was held as well. The performances by Yuzuru, Mao

■reconstruction 图復興 ■clown 图ピエロ ■segment 图 (プログラムなど の) ひとコマ ■mingle 動交流する ■temporary residence 仮設住宅

そんな時、「少しでも滑る機会になれば」と、このオフシーズンにアイスショーに参加しないかという声がかかり、4月9日の神戸の復興支援アイスショーからの出演が決まった。

　「自分を助けて、スケートを続けさせてくれる人がたくさんいることに感謝しました」

　アイスショーというのは、様々な団体が主催し、国内外の現役選手、ジュニアの上位選手、プロスケーターなどが参加し、全国各地で開催されるエンターテインメント性のある興行のこと。歌手のナマ歌や生演奏、ダンスバトルがあったり、クラウン（ピエロ）や空中の曲芸や選手とのふれあいタイムもあったりする。この年は、いくつものアイスショーが協力して「復興支援アイスショー」を約60回、全国各地で開催した。

　その一つに、7月27日に青森県八戸市の新井田インドアリンクで開催された「THE ICE」がある。東北3県から仮設住宅暮らしの1400名を無料招待。子どもたちへのスケート教室も実施した。結弦をはじめ浅田真央や小塚崇彦、さらに海外のトップスケーターによる演技がショーを盛り上げた。その中でも結弦

Asada, Takahiko Kozuka and top skaters from abroad were well received by the audience. Yuzuru, in particular, made a profound impression on the people who were there. He performed the latter half of "Romeo and Juliet" with no mistakes, and he appeared on the rink several times and talked to the victims of the disaster. In the finale, in answer to the audience who would not stop applauding after the other performers had gone, Yuzuru came back onto the ice and demonstrated some clean jumps. The audience responded to him enthusiastically.

A victim of the disaster and a skater

Yuzuru practiced during the break times of the ice shows. And at the shows, he tried out various programs and refined them. "White Legend (from Swan Lake)," which he performed for his SP after he entered the senior level, was one of them. This piece composed by Tchaikovsky was arranged by Ikuko Kawai, a violinist. Yuzuru wore a costume with white feathers, and put on black gloves. This beautiful program put an emphasis on the skating rather than the jumps. Usually, this type of music was seen as more suitable for female skaters, but when Yuzuru performed it with amazing flexibility, and thanks to his neutral face and slender body, this distinction did not matter anymore.

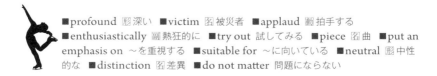
■profound 形深い ■victim 名被災者 ■applaud 動拍手する ■enthusiastically 副熱狂的に ■try out 試してみる ■piece 名曲 ■put an emphasis on ～を重視する ■suitable for ～に向いている ■neutral 形中性的な ■distinction 名差異 ■do not matter 問題にならない

は、観客に深い印象を与えた。『ロミオ＋ジュリエット』の後半部分をノーミスで演じただけでなく、たびたびリンクに登場し、被災者へのメッセージを語った。フィナーレでは、他の出演者が退場してもなお拍手を続ける観客に応えるため、リンクに戻って鮮やかなジャンプを決めて大きな喝采を浴びた。

被災者としての自分とスケーターとしての自分

　結弦は、アイスショーの幕間の時間を使って練習するとともに、ショーでは、さまざまなプログラムを試し、洗練させる場にした。シニアになってからSPで使っていた『白鳥の湖 〜ホワイト・レジェンド〜』の振付けがそれだ。チャイコフスキーの曲をヴァイオリニスト川井郁子がアレンジした曲だ。黒手袋に白い羽根がついた衣装をまとい、ジャンプよりもスケーティングを重視した美しいプログラムである。曲想的には女性向きと思えるが、中性的な面立ちと細長い体型そして驚くほどの柔軟さで演じると、そんなことは気にならない。

For this program, he stretched his arms on the ice, and began his performance in a lower sitting position. Then, he gradually woke up, paused like a bird with flapping wings, and executed some "donut spins" (the spin is called a donut because the skater's body looks like one while rotating with one raised leg touching the head). He looked as if he was a rotating white swan on the water. Then he lowered his body as far as it could go to do a sitting spin. This was followed by a long "twizzle," which is a multi-rotational turn on one foot. The last sequence started with a "Biellmann spin," which is a catch-foot position where the free leg is pulled above the head from behind, then he did a sitting spin and stood to do the finishing pose. In this program, all his techniques were connected smoothly, his body flexibility stood out, and it gave an elegant impression overall.

"I tend to go deeper inside myself when I try to express my feelings. But with this music, I tried to express the feelings inside of me outside of myself and show them to the world. And I performed this program with an image in my mind of the affected area rising up," said Yuzuru.

He continued to use this piece at competitions after this, and performed this program in his exhibition performance after the 2014 Sochi Olympics where he won the gold medal.

■wake up 目覚める　■as if まるで〜のように　■as far as it can 〜できる極限まで　■sequence 图 (一連の) シーン　■stand out 際立つ　■tend to 〜しがちである

氷上に両手を前に伸ばし、しゃがんだうつ伏せの形から入る。ゆっくり目覚めて、羽ばたくようなポーズしてからのドーナツ・スピン（挙げた片足を後ろから頭につけて回転するとドーナツが回っているように見える）。まさに水上で回る白鳥に見える。そこから体を極限まで沈めるシット・スピンに移り、片足で多回転するツイヅルの時間も長い。ラストは背後から頭上に挙げた足のブレードを持ってのビールマン・スピンからシットにして、立ち上がってフィニッシュのポーズに入る。技がスムースに繋がり、体の柔らかさが際立ち、華麗な印象を受ける。

　「自分は、感情を出そうとすると内面に深く入ってしまうのですが、この曲では、感情をカタチにして外に出そうとしました。そして、被災地が立ち上がる姿をイメージして演技をしました」

　この曲は、以後の試合でも使い続け、2014年のソチ五輪優勝後のエキシビションにもこれを演じた。

Right after the disaster and a few years after that, wherever he went he was treated as "the representative of the victims of the disaster," and was asked the same questions about the disaster over and over again. Whenever he was asked those questions, he answered as follows:

"Even though I'm a victim of the disaster, I'm doing my best as you can see. I'm glad if you feel that this is the best I can do." But gradually, he started to feel that something was not right.

He wondered: by appearing in front of the audience as a skater, I could give hope to the people in the affected area. This may have been a very good and correct answer, but he was not sure if these were really his own words. Should he rather do some volunteer work for the reconstruction? Or what he should do was skating for the second year as a senior-level figure skater? As he was grateful to the situations that he could come back to skating, he thought he should fulfill his responsibility as a skater representing Japan. He started to see more clearly what he had to do.

In July, his home rink "Ice Rink Sendai" reopened, and soon the 2011–2012 season started. Yuzuru was determined to win and decided to perform quadruple jumps in the FS and SP as well. His success rate was still low, but he would not be able to win at the Japan Championships without doing them. Debuting at the World Championships and participating in the Sochi Olympics three

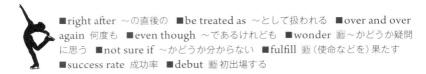

■right after 〜の直後の　■be treated as 〜として扱われる　■over and over again 何度も　■even though 〜であるけれども　■wonder 動〜かどうか疑問に思う　■not sure if 〜かどうか分からない　■fulfill 動 (使命などを) 果たす　■success rate 成功率　■debut 動 初出場する

震災の直後はもちろんのこと、数年の間、出かけて行く先々で、結弦は、「被災者の代表」のように扱われ、何度も同じような質問を受けた。そのたびにこう答えてきた。

　「被災しても、こうやって頑張っています。精一杯やっている姿を感じてもらえたらうれしいです」と。しかし、しだいに違和感もおぼえるようになってきていた。
　スケーターとしての自分の姿を見てもらうことが被災地を勇気づけることになる、というのは優等生的だが、本当に自分で考えた言葉なのかと迷った。やるべきことは復興ボランティアだろうか？　むしろ、シニア2年目のフィギュアスケーターとしての自分に徹するべきではないか？　スケートできる状態になれたことに感謝して、日本代表のスケーターとしての責任を果たすべきだろう……。そして結弦の心は迷いから抜け出していく。

　夏7月、ホームリンクの「アイスリンク仙台」が営業を再開した。2011-2012のシーズン・イン。結弦は「勝ちたい」という気持ちを高めて、自分の課題として、4回転ジャンプをフリー（FS）だけでなくショート（SP）にも取り入れることに定めた。まだ成功率は高くないが、これができなければ全日本選手権で勝てない。初の世界選手権にも出場できず、3年後のソチ五輪出場など

years after that would become just a dream if he did not include them. He really had to do it. It would be very heavy pressure on him. But as he had educated himself over the years to think positively, he could think of this pressure as the way to achieve his next steps.

Debuts at World Championships and wins bronze with a miracle performance

In September, Yuzuru participated in the Nebelhorn Trophy in Oberstdorf, Germany. As it is the first international senior competitions of the season, it is regarded as a gateway to success and a challenger series for the young skaters who are debuting at the senior level. Nobunari Oda won in 2008 and Tatsuki Machida won in 2010. And that year, Yuzuru won. This win was a good start for him.

On November 4 and 5, Yuzuru landed his first quadruple jump at the Cup of China, but he fell on his favorite triple axel in his FS and placed fourth. But after he analyzed the cause of the defeat, he realized that the difference between his scores and the top ones was only 1.96 points. He started the habit of having a "self-review meeting." He thought, "Just having a fighting spirit is not enough.

■educate oneself 覚える　■be regarded as ～とされている　■gateway 图入り口　■analyze 動分析する　■defeat 图敗北

夢の彼方に消えてしまう。絶対、後には引けないのだ。大変な
プレッシャーになるのは当然だが、プレッシャーを、「これがで
きれば、次はここまで行ける」というプラス思考に変えるのは、
結弦がいつしか身につけたスタイルだった。

世界選手権初出場、奇跡の演技で銅メダル

　9月、ドイツのオーベルストドルフで開催される「ネーベル
ホルン杯」に参加。シーズン最初の国際競技会のため初めてシ
ニアクラスに参加する若手たちの登竜門的な競技会、チャレン
ジャー・シリーズと位置づけられる。2008年には日本の織田信成
が、前年2010年には町田樹が優勝している。そしてこの年、結
弦が優勝。幸先の良いスタートになった。

　11月4〜5日、GPシリーズの中国杯はSPで初めて4回転に成
功しながら、FSで得意だったはずのトリプル・アクセルで失敗し
て4位。しかし、敗因を分析すると1位との総得点の差は1.96
点と僅差だった。この頃から習慣になった「ひとり反省会」では、
「闘争心だけではなく、冷静に最後まで演技に集中していたら勝
てたかもしれない」と考えた。

If I could have kept calm and concentrated on my performance till the end, I could have won."

On November 25 and 26, his next assigned Grand Prix Series was the Rostelecom Cup held in Moscow, Russia. In the previous year, he had finished seventh in this event. His quadruple jumps were not successful in the SP and FS, but he was able to maintain his "concentration power" and performed other jumps and spins cleanly. When he felt something was wrong with his jumps, he was able to change the program structure on the spot and recover from his mistakes. This was his first mature response. As a result, he won his first GP Series with an overall score of 241.66. The difference between the scores of Yuzuru and Javier Fernandez of Spain in second place was merely 0.03 points. Yuzuru thought that the reason for his win was his calmness in recovering from mistakes. With the fourth place at the Cup of China and this win, he qualified for his first senior GP Final.

On December 9 and 10, Yuzuru celebrated his 17th birthday in Canada. He was there for his debut in the GP Final in Quebec City. Only the six athletes with the highest scores in the GP Series in six countries can participate in this final. Those athletes were Patrick Chan of Canada, Daisuke Takahashi, Javier Fernandez, Jeremy Abbott of the United States and Michal Březina of the

■keep calm 冷静でいる　■assign 動（場所などを）決める　■concentration 名集中　■on the spot すぐにその場で　■merely 副ただ〜だけの　■celebrate 動祝う

同月25〜26日、続いてのGPは、去年7位になって悔しかったロシア・モスクワでのロステレコム杯。SP、FSとも4回転では失敗したものの、テーマにしていた「集中力」を切らさずに、他のジャンプもスピンもきれいに決めた。ジャンプの感覚が悪かった時にはすぐに演技の構成を変えてリカバリーしたことも、彼には初めての大人っぽい適応だった。結果、総合得点241.66でGP初優勝。2位のハビエル・フェルナンデス（スペイン）とは紙一重の0.03点差。リカバリーする冷静さがあったから勝てたと思った。中国杯の4位とこの優勝で、結弦はGPファイナルへの出場を決めた。

　12月9〜10日、17歳の誕生日はカナダで迎えた。ケベック・シティでのGPファイナル初参加である。この大会には世界6ヵ国でのGPシリーズでの得点上位6人だけが出場できる。カナダのパトリック・チャン、高橋大輔、ハビエル・フェルナンデス、米国のジェレミー・アボット、チェコのミハル・ブレジナ。いずれも高い技術と4回転ジャンプそして表現力を備えた超トップ

Czech Republic. All of them were super top athletes, and each had a high level of technique including quadruple jumps and superb expressiveness. Yuzuru was ranked sixth. He was able to beat his personal best overall score, but finished fourth behind Chan, Takahashi and Fernandez. A good thing that came out of this result was that he felt his performance level was getting closer to that of the top skaters.

The top-class skaters have no time to relax during December. On December 23 and 24, only two weeks after the GP Final in Canada, the Japan Championships started, which determine the top skater in Japan. Takahashi and other top male and female skaters including Mao Asada, Akiko Suzuki and Kanako Murakami participated in this event. Naturally, "Namihaya Dome" in Osaka was packed with fans for these two days. Although most of the flags and placards were for Takahashi, a few flags for "YUZU" could be seen. Yuzuru was glad to see that. But he made mistakes in his SP and finished third after Takahashi and Kozuka despite the fact that he came first in the FS. Still, he was able to earn a spot on the Japanese team for the World Championships in 2012.

■superb 形すばらしい　■expressiveness 名表現力　■beat 動打ち破る ■come out（結果などが）出る　■have no time to ～している時間はない　■be packed with ～でいっぱいである　■earn 動獲得する

選手。結弦のランクは6番目だった。結果からいえば、総得点で自分の記録を更新できたものの、チャン、高橋、フェルナンデスに負けて4位。超トップたちとの差が少しは縮まったと思えたことが収穫だった。

　同月23〜24日、この時期、トップクラスのスケーターたちにはゆっくり休める時間がない。カナダでのGPファイナルからわずか2週間で、今度は国内でのトップを決める全日本選手権になる。高橋を筆頭に層の厚い日本男子と女子では浅田真央、鈴木明子、村上佳菜子たちが競うのだから、会場となった大阪「なみはやドーム」は、期間中ファンたちで超満員になった。応援の旗やプラカードは圧倒的に高橋ファンのものだったが、「YUZU」の旗も少し見えるようになった。その応援に喜んだものの、SPでのミスがたたり、FSで首位になったものの高橋、小塚に負けての3位。何とか、翌年のワールドチャンピオンシップ（世界選手権）への出場資格を獲得した。

In March 2012, Yuzuru debuted in the World Championships in Nice, France, as the youngest Japanese male. He placed seventh in the SP. And, despite a sprained right ankle, he came back from behind by performing a miraculous FS program "Romeo and Juliet" and won the bronze medal behind Chan and Takahashi with a total score of 251.06. Until that point, often he didn't have enough stamina left at the end of the program, and would fall over when doing a triple Salchow. But this time, he was successful. For his fighting spirit and coming through the difficult experience as a victim of a disaster, he received huge applause and a standing ovation from the crowd. He could not move for three seconds after the finish as he had tears in his eyes.

During that season, Yuzuru struggled but was able to gain the ability to score steadily.

"I thought I'd been skating to lift the spirit of the disaster affected area. But I was wrong. I was the one who received an uplift of spirit. Many fans came all the way to Nice to support me. There were also many fans watching on TV. I have realized that the best way to show my gratitude is to perform while accepting the warm support from my fans," he said in a review of that season.

■despite 前 ~にもかかわらず ■sprain 動 ねん挫する ■miraculous 形 奇跡の ■come through（困難などを）耐え抜く ■applause 名 拍手 ■struggle 動 苦労して進む ■uplift of spirit 元気が出ること ■gratitude 名 感謝

明けて2012年3月、フランス・ニースでの世界選手権に日本男子最年少として初出場。右足首をねん挫しながらも、SP7位からFSで奇跡の演技（曲目は『ロミオ＋ジュリエット』）で挽回し、チャンと高橋に続き総合251.06で3位銅メダルとなった。これまで終盤になるとスタミナが落ちて、失敗しがちだった「3回転サルコウ」を決めたのだ。震災の被災にもめげずに戦い抜いた結弦の気迫に対して、会場は大きな拍手とスタンディング・オベーションで報いた。3秒間フィニッシュの姿のまま立ち尽くした結弦の眼に涙があった。

　試合後、結弦は苦しかったものの着実に得点力を高めることができたこのシーズンを、こう振り返った。
　「被災地を元気づけるためにと思って滑ってきたけど、それは違う。逆にボクが元気をもらう立場だったのです。このニースにまで応援に来てくれるファンの方々もいる。TVの向こうでも応援してもらっている。その応援を受け止めて演技することが一番の恩返しだと気づきました」

☙Column 2❧ The difference between the short program (SP) and free skating (FS)

In figure skating, a skater is judged not only by the skating techniques as an athlete in terms of the accuracy of their skating techniques and the difficulty level of the performance, but also as an artist in terms of their ability of expression and understanding of the accompanying music. Therefore, the opinions of the judges matter a lot and this often leads to criticism and dissatisfaction with their judgments. To judge more objectively, the International Skating Union (ISU) has been leading the way in the discussions on how to improve the judging system. Some changes have been implemented as a result of these efforts. For instance, the term "technical program," which was used up to 1994, was changed to "short program (SP)." And from the 2004–2005 season, the judging system was changed to the current ISU judging system. There will be minor changes in the system going forward, but the judging standards that have been deployed as of fall in 2017 are as follows (with some differences in the judging standards for male and female, and for junior and senior skaters). Below are the judging standards for male seniors:

The SP is performed first. Everybody skates using the same techniques. The skater has free choice in the selection of the music. During the SP, which is two minutes 40 seconds (plus or minus 10 seconds) in duration, the following elements have to be included in the performance:

1) One axel jump; 2) one independent triple or quadruple jump; 3) a combination jump that must be different from the jump in 2; 4) a flying spin; 5) a spin with another foot; 6) a combination spin; and 7) a step sequence. In the step sequence, several kinds of steps and

〔コラム2〕 SPとFSの違い

　フィギュアでは、演技の難易度や正確性などアスリートとしてのスケーティング技術だけでなく、表現力や曲想の理解力などアーティストとしての側面も評価の対象になる。したがって審査員の主観が入りやすくなり、評価への批判や不満も生じやすくなる。評価をより客観的に行おうとして、ISU（国際スケート連盟）などが中心になって、評価方法の検討と改善を重ねてきた。1994年までは「テクニカル・プログラム」と称してきたものがSPに変更され、2004−2005年シーズンからは現在のISUジャッジングシステムになったのもそうした取り組みの一つである。今後も細かい変更はあると思われるが2017年秋までに実施されている基準は以下のようになっている。ただ、男子と女子、ジュニアとシニアでは少し異なるので、ここでは男子シニアのものとする。

　まずSP。これは全員が同じ技を滑る。曲目は自由に選べる。持ち時間2分40秒±10秒の間に、①アクセルジャンプを1回、②単独の3ないし4回転ジャンプを1回、③②のジャンプとは異なる種類のコンビネーション・ジャンプ、④フライング・スピン、⑤足を換えてのスピン、⑥コンビネーション・スピン、⑦ステップ・シークエンスという要素を必ず盛り込んだものを滑らなくてはならない。ステップ・シークエンスというのは、音楽の特徴に合わせて複数のステップやターンを組み合わせ、氷上に図形を描きながら移動する演技でリンク全面を使う。

turns are combined to match the characteristics of the music, and the athlete skates while drawing figures on the ice using all the area of the rink.

Next, the FS is performed. Again, the skater can choose their music. During the FS, which lasts four minutes 30 seconds (plus or minus 10 seconds), the following must be included:

1) Up to eight jumps in total including at least one axel; 2) a maximum of three spin combinations; and 3) one step sequence, and at the end, a choreographic sequence consisting of various kinds of movements. For this one, there is no level judgment, and it is judged by fixed base value and a GOE (which stands for grade of execution.) The GOE is added to the base value to get judging panel's score for each element. In the FS, the skater has a longer performance time and has more freedom in the choice of combinations than in the SP. The program components score accounts for twice as much as in the SP. Also, the FS accounts for a larger percentage of the total score.

As explained above, in the SP and FS, the score is determined by awarding set points for each technique and a GOE score, which is a judgment on the overall performance, with deductions for falls and insufficient rotations. A big difference between the junior and senior levels is that the performance time for seniors is as much as 30 seconds longer than that for juniors. In normal life, 30 seconds is short, but it is really long in the world of athletes who perform with all their power. Yuzuru had performed really well in junior championships. But when he first skated at the senior level, he faced great difficulty in maintaining his stamina until the end. As he has asthma, he even practiced with a mask on to improve his lung capacity.

次に FS。曲目は自由に選べる。持ち時間 4 分 30 秒 ± 10 秒の間に、①最低 1 つのアクセルジャンプを含む合計 8 つまでのジャンプ、②スピン・コンビネーションは最大 3 回、③ステップ 1 回、最後にあらゆる種類の動作から構成されるコレオグラフィック・シークエンスがある。これはレベル判定がなく、固定された基礎点と GOE のみで評価される。

　GOE というのは、「Grade of Execution」の略称で、それぞれの要素がどれだけの出来だったかを評価するものである。SP と違うのは、長い演技時間と組合せの自由度が高いこと、演技構成点がショートの 2 倍入る。総得点に占める割合は FS が大きい。

　ということで SP と FS は、「技ごとに与えられる基礎点＋できばえ評価の GOE、そしては転倒や回転不足に対する減点（ディダクション）」によって得点が決められる。なお、ジュニアとの違いで大きいのは、シニアの演技時間が 30 秒も長いことだ。この 30 秒の差は普通の生活では短いようだが、全力で演技するアスリートの世界ではとても長い。ジュニアの大会で活躍してきた結弦も、シニアの大会に臨んだ初めの頃は、終盤のスタミナ切れに随分悩まされた。喘息の持病もある結弦は、肺活量を高めるためにマスクを着けたままでの練習さえ行った。

覚えておきたい英語表現

The sound of shaking was really loud and beyond my imagination.
（p. 44, 最終行）
揺れている音は本当に大きくて僕の想像を超えていた。

　Beyondは「〜を超えて」「〜の向こう側に」という意味で広く知られる前置詞です。慣用的に使われることも多く、ぜひたくさんの表現で慣れておきたい言葉です。

　　　　He wanted to go beyond the borders.
　　　　彼は国境を越えたいと思っていた。

　　　　She lived beyond her income.
　　　　彼女は収入以上の生活をしていた。

　beyondは「はるかに超えている」イメージを持つので……

　　　　This theory is beyond me.　　私にはこの理論は分からない。

　　　　This beautiful scenery is beyond my description.
　　　　（直訳）この美しい風景は私の描写（力）を超えている。
　　　　（意訳）この美しい光景は言い表せない。

　などの使い方もあります。本文のbeyond my imaginationもこれに近いですね。少々固く聞こえますが、感動や驚きを伝える表現を多く知っておくことはコミュニケーションにおいてとても大事です。ぜひ使いこなしてください。

> If I could have kept calm and concentrated..., I could have won.
> （p. 60, 1行目）
> 冷静さと集中力を保てたなら、勝つことができたのに。

　仮定法過去完了が用いられていて、羽生選手の悔しい気持ちがよく伝わってくる英文です。

　仮定法はとても難解で、苦手に感じる方がとても多い文法です。覚えておくべきなのは「仮定法過去」と「仮定法過去完了」という二つの文法です。

【仮定法過去の例文】

　　I wish I *could* play the piano.
　　ピアノが弾けたらなあ。

　本当はピアノを弾くことはできないのですが、「ピアノを弾くことができるならいいのに」という、「現在の事実に反する」気持ちや行動を「過去形」で表現するので仮定法過去と言います。

【仮定法過去完了】

　　I wish I could have passed the exam.
　　あの試験に合格していたならなあ。

　過去の時点で試験には合格できなかったのですが、「もしあの時合格していたならなあ」という、「過去の事実に反する」気持ちや行動を「過去完了形（had＋Vpp）」で表現します。助動詞が過去形couldになっていて、hadはその後ろに来るため原形にします。

　仮定法に慣れると、英語を奥深く楽しむことができるようになります。羽生選手の物語を読み進めながら、仮定法を見つけるたびにその文法に込められた気持ちを読み取ってみてください。

Part 3

Training
in Canada

カナダでトレーニング

Training abroad: selecting a coach and learning new things

After the last competition of the previous season, which was the World Championships in Nice where Yuzuru became the bronze medalist, his coach Nanami Abe told him, "Let's open your eyes more to the world. You should have a coach outside Japan." In the world of sports and arts, when one reaches a certain level, it is not unusual to travel abroad to learn from a coach in a country where certain knowledge and technologies are more advanced in the particular field you are in. Abe thought it was the right time for Yuzuru to do that because he had been scoring more steadily and ranking high regularly in big competitions in Japan and other countries.

Yuzuru was hesitant about leaving his beloved family, his coach and Sendai, but he understood what the coach meant. He thought about a new coach and the things he wanted to learn from that person. He knew his artistic expression was not yet good enough. Should he learn how to improve the program components score? If so, should he go to Russia with which he had an affinity and where Plushenko lived? However, thinking back, what had motivated

■reach a certain level ある一定のレベルに達する ■advanced 形 進歩的な
■particular field 専門分野 ■steadily 副 安定して ■hesitant 形 ためらって
■affinity 名 親近感

留学で、「誰に、何を学ぶべきか」

　前シーズン最後の試合、銅メダルになったニースでの世界選手権の後で、阿部奈々美コーチは結弦に、「これからは海外にもっと目を向けましょう。海外の先生に見てもらいましょう」と言った。スポーツや芸術の世界では、あるレベルに達すると、より進んだ国の指導者の元に留学することは珍しくない。阿部コーチは、着実に点数を伸ばし、国内外の大きな大会でも安定して上位入賞するようになった結弦にも、そのタイミングに来たと判断してのアドバイスだった。

　結弦は、大好きな家族、コーチ、仙台と離れることをためらったが、コーチの言葉も理解した。そして「誰に、何を学ぶべきか」と考えた。芸術的な表現力が弱いと思っていたから、演技構成点を上げる勉強をすべきか？　それなら自分の感覚にも合い、プルシェンコらがいるロシアだろうか？　いや、今まで自分が一番成長の糧にしてきたのは、次々と現れるライバルたちの演技だった。彼らは、芸術面だけでなく、スピードや正確さ、

his advancement the most had been the performances of various rivals one after another. They stimulated him with their brilliant talent, not only from the artistic perspective, but also in terms of their speed, accuracy and powerfulness as well. Considering all these things, he had an inclination to be near his current rival. In particular, he was thinking of Javier Fernandez, a Spanish skater born in 1991. Fernandez had made a strong impression on Yuzuru at Yuzuru's first GP Final in Canada the previous year. Yuzuru knew that Fernandez trained in Canada and his performance had improved rapidly under a good coach. That coach was Brian Orser. He is known for having trained Yuna Kim, a gold medalist at the 2010 Vancouver Olympics.

Yuzuru made up his mind. And soon after that, he asked if he could contact Orser and then met him. He communicated with Orser in English even though his English was poor. He said to Orser, "I want to go to Toronto, and work with Brian." Orser understood his firm determination and told him, "Team Brian will welcome you."

■one after another 次々と　■perspective 名視点　■in terms of ～の観点から　■accuracy 名正確さ　■inclination 名意向　■think of ～が心に浮かぶ　■make up one's mind 心を決める　■ask if one could ～してもいいか聞く　■firm 形断固とした

力強さなどそれぞれに光る才能を持っていて、自分を刺激して
くれた。ということは、今の自分がライバルと思える選手の近
くに行くのが良いかもしれない……。結弦の脳裏に浮かんだの
は、昨年、初挑戦のGPファイナル（カナダ）で強い印象を受けた
1991年生まれのスペイン人選手ハビエル・フェルナンデスだっ
た。彼はカナダに留学して、良い指導者の下で急成長したこと
を知っていた。フェルナンデスを教えているコーチは、ブライ
アン・オーサー。2010年のバンクーバー五輪で韓国女子のキム・
ヨナを金メダルに導いたことで知られている。

　結弦の心は決まった。早速、オーサーに連絡をとってもらっ
て会うことになり、拙い英語でその意思を伝えた。「I want to
go to Toronto, and work with Brian」。結弦の真剣さを認めて、
オーサーは「チーム・ブライアンは君を歓迎するよ」と応えてく
れた。

There was a reason why Orser said "Team Brian" instead of "I." In Japan, it is common that one coach teaches very few athletes, and no other coaches are involved. But Brian Orser has a team of about 20 coaches, 60 top athletes and 400 farm skaters. As a head coach, Brian Orser acts as a director, Tracy Wilson is in charge of skating techniques and David Wilson oversees choreography. Also, there are many other specialists in his team such as Paige Aistrop who is an ISU technical controller, athletic trainers, sports masseurs and contracted doctors.

Here is what Orser thinks about Team Brian: "For figure skating nowadays, a lot of complicated and specialized knowledge is required. By having the best specialists in each field, we can offer the best support system. What I can do alone is limited. When I coach an athlete to win, I take responsibility for all of his or her life as an athlete. It is also important to give advice or care for an athlete's mental health. I change coaches if necessary. Like operating a company, management is necessary in our team."

His home base is the "Toronto Cricket Skating and Curling Club" located in Toronto, Canada. People can enjoy cricket and curling as well as figure skating there. It is a prestigious club with a gorgeous club house.

■instead of ～ではなく　■farm 图ファーム、二軍　■act as ～の役を務める
■masseur 图マッサージ師　■complicated 形複雑な　■take responsibility
for ～に関して責任を負う　■care for ～への配慮　■operate 動経営する
■located in ～に位置する　■prestigious 形名門の

オーサー個人でなく「チーム・ブライアン」と言ったのには理由がある。日本の一般的なリンクでは、1人のコーチがごく少数の選手を指導することが多く、他のコーチは関与しない。しかし、ブライアン・オーサーのやり方は、約20人のコーチ陣と、約60人のトップ選手、その下の約400人のファーム・スケーターまで含めた全員を1つのチームとしている。ヘッド・コーチのブライアン・オーサーはまとめ役、スケーティング技術ならトレーシー・ウィルソン、振付けはデヴィッド・ウィルソン、ISUの技術役員資格を持つペイジ・アイストロップ、他にも陸上トレーナー、マッサージ師、契約ドクターもいるといった具合である。

　「今のフィギュアは、複雑で専門的な知識がたくさん必要だ。各分野の最高の専門家を集めることで最高のサポート体制ができる。私ができることは限られている。そして選手を勝たせるためには、その競技人生を引き受けるつもりでコーチングする。スケート以外の相談や、メンタル面のケアも大切で、必要ならコーチも変更する。会社経営と同じくマネジメントが必要だ」というのが、オーサーの考え方なのだ。

　その本拠地こそ、カナダ・トロントにある「トロント・クリケット・スケーティング＆カーリングクラブ」である。フィギュアだけでなくクリケットやカーリングも楽しめる、豪華なクラブハウスを持った名門クラブだ。

Re-learning the skating fundamentals

When Yuzuru moved to Canada, he was just thinking that it would be nice if he could see Fernandez's quadruple jumps in person. But Orser ordered him to "restructure the basics of skating." According to him, "skating techniques are the fundamentals of figure skating." Yuzuru had been skating for more than 10 years. So basic training might not have been what he wanted to do every day. But when he looked back at his past practice, it kind of made sense to him. In Sendai, he could only do basic skating practice to strengthen his lower body during the off-season in the summer. Within this limited practice time, most of his time was spent on practicing the big elements of the program with music as preparation for real competitions. Despite these poor conditions for basic training, he had still been able to accomplish a lot as a skater thanks to his former coach Tsuzuki's thorough basic training when he was a young boy.

Tracy Wilson, one of the head coaches, was in charge of Yuzuru's basic training. She was an ice dance medalist at the 1988 Calgary Olympics. Under Wilson's direction, Yuzuru focused on the "stroking technique." This is just a simple motion in which

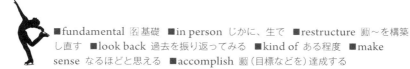
■fundamental 名基礎 ■in person じかに、生で ■restructure 動～を構築し直す ■look back 過去を振り返ってみる ■kind of ある程度 ■make sense なるほどと思える ■accomplish 動（目標などを）達成する

基礎のスケーティングから学び直し

　「フェルナンデスの4回転が見られたらいい」という気持ちでカナダに拠点を移した結弦だったが、オーサーから与えられた課題は、「スケーティングを基礎から作り直す」というものだった。オーサーによれば、「スケーティング技術こそすべての基本」というのだ。これまでに10年以上もスケートをやってきた結弦にすれば、毎日、基礎の練習ばかりさせられるのは不本意だったかもしれない。しかしよく考えれば思い当たることもある。仙台で、主に下半身を鍛えるスケーティングの基礎練習は、夏場のオフの時しかできなかった。限られた練習時間は、本番の試合に向けて曲をかけて大技の練習をするだけで過ぎてしまっていた。それでもここまで来られたのは、幼い時に都築コーチらが基礎をみっちり仕込んでくれたからでもある。

　結弦の基礎トレーニングを担当したのはもう一人のヘッド・コーチ、トレーシー・ウィルソンだった。1988年のカルガリー五輪アイス・ダンスのメダリストだ。ウィルソンに指導されてストローキングをやってみる。右脚と左脚を交互に出して前進する

the skater moves forward using the right and left foot alternately. But by doing it while paying special attention to the balance of his body or the movement of his legs, he was able to feel his sense of touch on the ice or his skating speed more sensitively. While practicing foot work with a group of 20 people, Yuzuru could see himself in a mirror on the wall and noticed that his motion was the least smooth among them. He was not able to use the edges of the blades at a deep enough angle to move expansively and quickly. But Yuzuru's character did not allow him to become depressed. On the contrary, he decided to accept Orser and Wilson's coaching wholeheartedly. Anticipating that it might become a big chance for him, he felt excited. He rediscovered the joy of skating.

Yuzuru was looking forward to practicing jumps, and this started at the same time as the basic training. Orser was born in Canada in 1961. He is the 1984 (Sarajevo) and 1988 (Calgary) Olympics silver medalist. He is also the 1987 World Championships winner. He could execute the most difficult level of jumps at that time, and was called "Mr. Triple Axel." He is a coach who well knows what is needed for jumps, and who also knows the frustration of being second best as well. He does not force his style on a skater he is coaching. He considers each athlete's body and muscle strength, and extends each one's personality. He videotaped the jumps of Yuzuru and Fernandez,

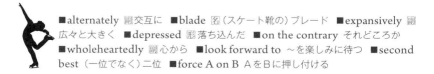

■alternately 副交互に　■blade 名（スケート靴の）ブレード　■expansively 副広々と大きく　■depressed 形落ち込んだ　■on the contrary それどころか　■wholeheartedly 副心から　■look forward to ～を楽しみに待つ　■second best（一位でなく）二位　■force A on B AをBに押し付ける

だけの動きだが、重心の動かし方や脚のさばき方を意識してやってみると、氷との密着感、スピードが違ってくる。20人ほどの集団でリンクを滑るフットワーク練習では、一番ぎこちない動きをしている自分が壁面の鏡に映っていた。大きく速く進むために必要になる、エッジを深く傾けて氷を押し出す動作ができていなかったのだ。しかし、こういうことで落ち込まないところが結弦の性格である。逆に、オーサーやウィルソンの指導を、全面的に受け入れようという気持ちがはっきりしてきた。自分のスケートを変える大きな転機になることに胸がわくわくした。スケートの楽しさを再発見したのだ。

　期待していたジャンプの練習も並行して始まった。1961年カナダ生まれのオーサー自身が84年のサラエボと88年のカルガリー五輪の銀メダリスト。87年の世界選手権では優勝しており、当時最高難度のジャンプ技を得意として「Mr.トリプル・アクセル」と呼ばれた人である。ジャンプに必要なことを熟知していると共に、金メダルに届かなかった悔しさも知っている指導者だった。その指導法は、自分のスタイルを押し付けない。選手それぞれの持つ体型や筋力を考え、個性を伸ばすやり方だった。結弦のジャンプを撮影し、フェルナンデスの映像と比較したりしながら、理論的にアドバイスする。これは視覚的なイメージ・トレーニングを重視する結弦には効果的だった。自分のジャンプ

and gave him theoretical advice by comparing their videos. This was very effective as Yuzuru preferred visual image training himself. He could learn about his habits while jumping and also came to understand the difference between successful jumps and failed ones both theoretically and visually.

 ## Thinking about the program for the new season

In his first summer in Toronto, to prepare for the 2012–2013 season, Yuzuru suggested the following idea to Orser:

"Only two seasons are left until the Sochi Olympics. I will be 19 then. So I will be expected to perform in a more mature way than I do now. To be able to do that, I think I have to start preparing from this season. It could be beyond my current level, but I'd like to try new expressions and more difficult skating."

Orser felt the same way and they decided to adopt this strategy right away. The person who would be in charge of Yuzuru's SP was Jeffrey Buttle. He was born in 1982. He retired after becoming the 2006 Winter Olympics bronze medalist in Turin and the 2008 World Championships winner. As for the FS, choreographer David Wilson, who was in charge of Yuna Kim and has an excellent artistic sense, was assigned to Yuzuru.

■theoretical 形 理論的な　■suggest 動 提案する　■be expected to　〜を期待される　■adopt 動 採用する　■right away　すぐに　■be assigned to　〜を担当する

の癖を知り、成功する時と失敗する時の違いを、理論と視覚イメージで学ぶことができた。

新シーズンの演技構成を考える

　トロントで迎えた最初の夏が過ぎれば、いよいよ2012−2013シーズンが開幕する。このシーズンにどう向かうべきかについて、結弦はオーサーにこう提案した。
　「ソチ五輪まであと2シーズンしかない。その時、ボクは19歳。今とは違う成熟した演技が求められることになるけど、それには今シーズンから準備しておかないと間に合わないと思う。少し背伸びしてでも新しい表現や難しい滑りに挑戦したい」
　オーサーも同感だったから、すぐにその作戦が決まった。SPを任せるのは、82年生まれで2006年のトリノで銅メダル、2008年の世界選手権で優勝して引退したジェフリー・バトル。FSは、キム・ヨナを担当したこともある芸術センス抜群の振付師、デヴィッド・ウィルソンが担当することになった。

Selecting the music is an important factor in figure skating. Yuzuru chose "Parisienne Walkways" for the SP. It is a song that was released by Gary Moore, an Irish guitarist, in 1978. It sounds like rock 'n' roll, but actually it is a ballad. Yuzuru had strong ideas about the jump combinations. He wanted to take into consideration the scoring system in which the jumps in the latter half of the performance, when a skater gets tired, can get 1.1 times more points than the ones in the first half.

"I want to do my favorite triple axel in the latter half of the performance. And to the jump starting from steps, I want to add a quadruple toe loop. I want them to be very high-level jumps," he said.

Average skaters would not include high-level jumps in the latter half of a program, considering the fatigue. Also, a certain amount of skating is necessary before jumps. It is almost impossible to jump right after steps without doing some skating first.

Orser and the other coaches were concerned about Yuzuru's bold suggestion. But Yuzuru was adamant. Besides, there was no advantage in him selecting just an ordinary and safe program at this point. They decided to go with Yuzuru's idea.

選曲も重要なテーマになる。SPは『パリの散歩道』。1978年に
アイルランドのギタリスト、ゲイリー・ムーアが発表したロック
調だがバラードの楽曲だ。SPのジャンプ構成には結弦が積極的
に提案した。演技時間の後半は、選手の疲れを考えて得点に1.1
倍のボーナスが加算されることを計算に入れようというのだ。

　「得意のトリプル・アクセルを後半に入れる。ステップから跳
ぶジャンプに4回転トゥ・ループを入れる。とにかくぎりぎり難
しいジャンプにしたい」

　並みの選手は、疲れるから後半に高難度の技はいれない。ま
た、ジャンプする際にはそれなりの助走を取る。助走なしでス
テップからそのままジャンプするのは、至難の技である。
　結弦の無謀な提案にオーサーもコーチ陣も心配した。しかし、
結弦は本気だったし、今さら平凡で安全なプログラムを選ぶ理
由はない。結弦の案を応援することに決まった。

For the FS, they decided to use songs from "Notre-Dame de Paris," a hit musical worldwide in 1998, which is based upon Victor Hugo's novel. The musical is famous for its musical score by Riccardo Cocciante and the performance by Celine Dion. The team mixed four songs from the musical. But as the story and the songs are complicated and very deep, it was a little too much for Yuzuru. The choreography was complicated as well, and it didn't allow him any rest at all. Wilson insisted that it had to be performed not just as a program but "as a piece of art." And it had to be done with quadruple toe loop and Salchow.

If Yuzuru had said that he would prefer an easier program, this complaint and hesitation could have ended his skating life as an average athlete. But he thought, "It's difficult for sure. But I have to do it because everybody believes in me and made this program for me. Besides, doing this now would be better than trying something new after I am 20," and decided to accept this challenge positively.

■based upon ～に基づく　■musical score 楽譜　■rest 動休息する
■insist 動主張する　■hesitation 名尻込み　■for sure 確実に

一方、FSの方は『ノートルダム・ド・パリ』に決まった。ヴィクトル・ユーゴーの小説というより、1998年にミュージカル化されて世界的にヒットし、リシャール・コッシアンテの曲とセリーヌ・ディオンの歌が知られている。このうちの4曲をミックスしたのだが、ストーリーも曲も複雑・重厚で、結弦は少し持て余した。振付けも複雑で息をつく場がなかった。これを演じ切るだけでなく、「作品として見せる」レベルにしようというのがウィルソンの主張だった。しかも4回転のトゥ・ループとサルコウを入れて、だ。

　ここで不平や尻込みで、「もっと滑りやすいものに」と言っていたら結弦は並みの選手で競技人生を終わっていたかもしれない。「難しい。でも、ボクを信じて考えてくれたプログラムなのだからやり遂げるしかない。今、苦しんでおけば、20歳を過ぎてから新しい挑戦をするより良いはずだ」とポジティブに受け止めることにした。

A year of challenge that confirmed his growth as an athlete

The new season started smoothly. The test ground of his ability was the Finlandia Trophy that started on October 4, 2012. Although there were some problems with the SP, he won the gold medal. From October 19, the first Grand Prix Series of the season, Skate America was held in Kent, Washington, U.S.A.

In his SP "Parisienne Walkways," he attempted difficult techniques including the quadruple toe loop and succeeded in making all his jumps. His score, 95.07, was a new world record for the SP. As regards to his total score, there was the added bonus that his program components score was better than before along with the technical score. But in his FS, he repeatedly made mistakes in the jumps and he came third. However, he still got a silver medal. Takahiko Kozuka placed first and Tatsuki Machida came third. The podium was monopolized by Japanese skaters, but this did not matter to Yuzuru. He was trying to identify the cause of his failure. In his usual "self-review meeting," he analyzed the problem: "I tried to forget about the SP, which was much better than I had expected. But because I tried to forget about it too hard, I couldn't think about anything else. I should have told myself to

■test ground 実験の場　■attempt 動～に挑戦する　■as regards ～について は　■along with ～と併せて　■monopolize 動～を独占する　■identify 動～ を明らかにする　■cause 名原因

自分の成長を確認しながら挑んだ1年間

　新シーズンは好調に滑り出した。腕試しの舞台になったのは12年10月4日から開幕したフィンランディア杯。SPに課題を残したものの優勝。同月19日からは、GPシリーズの初戦「スケートアメリカ」がワシントン州ケントで開催された。

　SPの『パリの散歩道』では4回転トゥ・ループをはじめ、あえて難しい技に挑戦したすべてのジャンプに成功。得点95.07でSPの世界記録を更新した。技術点だけでなく演技構成点を伸ばせたことも収穫だった。しかし、FSはジャンプでミスを繰り返して3位。総合で銀メダル。優勝は小塚崇彦、3位は町田樹と日本勢による表彰台独占だったが、結弦はそんなことより自分の敗因を探った。恒例の「ひとり反省会」でこう総括した。

　「良すぎたSPのことを忘れようとしたのだけど、『忘れよう』を意識し過ぎて頭が真っ白になってしまった。『フリーに集中』と意識すべきだった。それにしてもSPとFSを切り替えるのは難しい。でも、誰もが同じ課題に向き合っているのだから負けも経験しておこう。そしてトロントに来て、どこまで成長できたのかを確かめてみよう」

concentrate on the FS. Now I realize how difficult it is to reset my mind from the SP to the FS. But as everybody faces this problem, it was a good thing to experience a failure. I will see how much I have grown after I moved to Toronto."

The opportunity to confirm his growth came at the sixth GP Series in November in Japan. The GP Series competitions are held approximately every week starting in the U.S., then in Canada, China, Russia and France. To qualify for the GP Final, a skater has to participate in two competitions in the series and his/her total points have to be in the top six. As Yuzuru already had 13 points, which put him in second place, he concentrated on the NHK Trophy. And it happened to be held near Sendai, his hometown, at the Sekisui Heim Super Arena. This arena was used as a morgue after the disaster. Near the entrance of the stadium, there were pictures of the athletes holding messages on display. Yuzuru's message was "Do every single thing with care, and bring everything together." On the banners at the stadium, the messages to express gratitude for encouragement and help for Tohoku stood out.

At this event, Yuzuru performed his SP with no mistakes and scored 95.32. He beat his own world record. At the next FS performance, after having learned about "concentrating on the

■happen to 期せずして～する ■morgue 图遺体安置所 ■do every single thing 一つ一つやる ■banner 图横断幕

自分の成長を確かめる機会は、11月の日本でのGPシリーズ第6戦になった。初戦のアメリカから始まって、カナダ、中国、ロシア、フランスとGPシリーズはほぼ1週間の間隔で開催されたが、集大成の12月のGPファイナルに出場するには、2つの大会に出て、合計得点の上位6人に入れば良い。すでに2位の13点を得ている結弦は、このNHK杯に照準を定めていた。しかも開催地は故郷・宮城県、仙台市に隣接する利府町の「セキスイハイムスーパーアリーナ」。震災時には遺体安置所になった場所でもある。会場の入り口近くには、選手たちが自分のメッセージボードを持って写っている写真が並ぶ。結弦のは「一つ一つを丁寧に、全てを一つに」とある。会場のバナーには東北への連帯と支援への感謝のメッセージが目立った。

　この試合で結弦は、SPでノーミスの演技をして95.32。自身の得点世界記録を更新した。「フリーに集中する」ことを学んだ翌日のFS演技では、4回転トゥ・ループを成功したが、後半に行く

FS," he successfully landed a quadruple toe loop. But as he went into the second half of the FS, it was apparent that his stamina was wearing out, and consequently he fell, fell on his backside or touched the ice with his hands. Despite this, he got a win overall and beat Daisuke Takahashi for the first time. The cheers from the audience at the stadium were predominantly for Takahashi. But after watching Yuzuru's SP on the previous day and his brave challenge on this day, many fans started to see his ability and growth, and rooted for him. He was thankful for his hometown fans.

By winning at the NHK Trophy, he was able to add 15 points to his score, and qualified for the GP Final. It was held in Sochi, Russia. The venue was the Iceberg Skating Palace where the Olympics would be held 14 months later, and this GP Final was a test run for the Olympics. Sochi is a resort city located on the Black Sea coast. But the area near the stadium was still under construction and most of the transportation system and facilities were not yet completed.

The day of his SP, December 7, was Yuzuru's 18th birthday. He wanted to give himself a present of becoming the top skater by beating his own record, but unfortunately he could not do it. He made consecutive mistakes with the jumps in the second half of the program, and placed third in the SP. In his FS the following

■apparent 形明らかな ■wear out ～を使い果たす ■consequently 副その結果として ■predominantly 副圧倒的に ■root for ～を応援する ■venue 名開催地 ■test run 試運転 ■transportation system 交通機関 ■facility 名施設

ほど体力の消耗は明らかになり、転倒や尻餅や手をつくなどした。しかし総合では、高橋大輔を初めて抜いて優勝した。会場の声援は圧倒的に高橋に向けられていたが、昨日のSPや今日の果敢なチャレンジャーぶりに、結弦の実力を、その成長ぶりをあらためて見届けて応援したファンも多かった。地元ならではのありがたさだった。

　NHK杯で優勝したことで持ち点に15点をプラスし、結弦は12月のGPファイナルに出場した。開催地はロシアのソチ。あと14ヵ月後には五輪が開催される会場「アイスバーグ・スケーティング・パレス」でのテスト・マッチである。ソチは黒海沿岸の保養地だが、会場周辺は開発途上で、交通機関も施設も未完成なものが目立った。

　SP当日の12月7日は結弦の18歳の誕生日だったが、「再度の自己記録更新でトップに」という"自分へのプレゼント"は叶わなかった。後半のジャンプでミスが続いて3位での発進になった。翌日のFSは、後半が良かった。トリプル・アクセル2本などジャンプが完璧だった。FSトップは同門のフェルナンデスで、

day, the latter half was great. His jumps including two triple axels were perfect. Fernandez, his fellow skater in Team Brian, came top followed by Yuzuru. Patrick Chan, whom Yuzuru regarded as his main rival, made several mistakes. The final result in descending order was Takahashi, Yuzuru and Chan. This was the first time that Yuzuru had got onto the podium at a GP Final.

Skaters must be really tough to win. On December 21, less than two weeks after Sochi, Yuzuru was at the Japan Championships rink in Hokkaido. Among the abundant and talented Japanese male figure skaters with eight years' age difference between the youngest and the oldest, at least 10 had the potential to win. But this Championships revealed a clear trend; that of a generational change from Takahashi, Oda and Kozuka who were born in the 1980s to Yuzuru and Takahito Mura who were born in the 1990s. Yuzuru came top in the SP and second in the FS. Takahashi was second in the SP and top in the FS. In terms of the overall score, Yuzuru was first followed by Takahashi and Mura. Although it was the first win for Yuzuru at the Japan Championships, he wasn't smiling like a new champion.

"I admire and respect Mr. Takahashi. I won this time because my SP was good. But I really don't feel that I am better than him," he said.

■followed by その後に〜が続く　■descending order 高い順、降順　■tough 形屈強な　■less than 〜に満たない　■abundant 形たくさんの　■reveal 動（隠れていたものを）明らかに見せる　■admire 動〜をすばらしいと思う

結弦はそれに続いた。一番のライバルと見ていたパトリック・チャンはミスが続いた。結果は、高橋、結弦、チャンの順になった。結弦にとってGPファイナル初の表彰台だった。

　スケート選手は本当にタフでなければ勝てない。ソチから2週間も経たない12月21日、結弦は北海道・真駒内の全日本選手権のリンクに立っていた。層の厚い日本人男子フィギュアは、8歳ほどの年齢差の中に誰が優勝してもおかしくない選手が10人はいた。しかし、90年代生まれの結弦や無良崇人らが、80年代生まれの高橋、織田、小塚らと世代交代する流れがはっきりと見えた大会になった。結果だけ書けば、結弦がSPで首位、FSで2位になり、高橋がSPで2位、FSで首位。総合得点差で結弦、高橋、無良の順になった。結弦の全日本選手権優勝は初めてだったが、新チャンピオンに笑顔はなかった。

　「高橋選手は、すべての面での憧れ、雲の上の存在です。ショートで良かったから勝てたけど、実力で抜いたという実感はありません」

The last two competitions of that season in 2013 were the Four Continents Championships in February and the World Championships in March. Yuzuru finished second and fourth, respectively. The winner of the Four Continents was Kevin Reynolds, who became the sixth person in history to successfully land on three quadruple jumps. Patrick Chan won the World Championships for the third year running. His score was higher than Yuzuru's record high score in the SP at the NHK Trophy. Denis Ten, a Korean Kazakhstani skater, placed second, and Fernandez, Yuzuru's fellow skater, came third.

There was good news other than skating for Yuzuru. He graduated from Tohoku High School and passed the entrance examination for the School of Human Sciences at Waseda University. It was a correspondence program called "e-school." He entered this school not on recommendation, but through taking a normal entrance examination by presenting a thesis and having an interview. It would not be easy both skate and study to graduate from college, but Yuzuru could do it with his fighting spirt and tenacity.

■respectively 副 それぞれ　■graduate from ～を卒業する　■pass 動 合格する　■entrance examination 入学試験　■recommendation 名 推薦　■tenacity 名 頑張り

このシーズンの最後は、年が明けた2013年2月の四大陸選手権と3月の世界選手権だった。そこでの成績は2位と4位。前者の優勝は史上6人目となる3度の4回転ジャンプを決めたカナダのケヴィン・レイノルズ、後者の優勝は3連覇を果たしたパトリック・チャンで、NHK杯で結弦が記録したSPの最高得点を抜いた。そして韓国系カザフスタン人のデニス・テンが2位、結弦と同門のフェルナンデスは3位に入った。

　スケート以外の朗報もあった。結弦が東北高校を卒業して早稲田大学人間科学部人間情報科学科に合格した。「eスクール」という通信教育課程だが、推薦ではなく論文と面接による通常の試験による入学だった。勉強と両立させて卒業するのは簡単ではないだろうが、持ち前の負けん気と頑張りをこの面でも見せてくれることだろう。

覚えておきたい英語表現

> It could be beyond my current level, (p. 84, 下から9行目)
> それは僕の現在のレベルを超えているのかもしれないけれども

beyondはPart2でも取り上げましたね。be beyond〜で「〜を超えている」という意味になります。

ここで注目いただきたいのはcouldの使い方です。過去のことを述べているわけではないのに、なぜcanではなくcouldを使っているのでしょうか？

> He could go to Tokyo this weekend.
> 彼は今週末東京に行くかもしれないよ。

> I suppose you could be wrong.
> 君の言っていることは間違っているかもしれないよ。

これらの表現は過去のことではなく、未来や現在のことを述べているにもかかわらず過去形couldが使われています。なぜ「過去形could」を使いたくなるのでしょう？

当たり前のことですが、過去に戻ることはできません。それゆえ過去形は「遠い」イメージを想起させます。そしてcanは「可能性」を示す助動詞なので「確信はないけど、もしかしたら〜かもしれない」という意味になるのです。「遠い」イメージは相手との心理的距離感を感じさせるので……

> Could you wait a moment, please?　ちょっと待っていただけますか？

というような丁寧な表現にも使われます。Can you 〜 ？よりも丁寧さが増すのです。

ちなみにPart2で取り上げた、仮定法もこの「過去形は遠い」というイメージに導かれる文法です。

> If I could play the piano, I would play the music for you.
> もしピアノが弾けるなら、その曲を君に弾いてあげるのに。

なぜ、現在の事実に反することを過去形で述べるのか？ それはピアノが弾けないという現状からすれば、「ピアノが弾ける自分」がいる世界は遠いからです。過去形を用いることで、遠い世界の話をすることができるのです。言い換えれば、現実離れした「遠い世界の」話をするため、過去形を用いたくなるのです。

　文法は単なる決まりやルールではありません。気持ちを伝える手段なのです。得てして文法学習はつまらないもののように言われがちですが、その文法に込められた話し手の気持ちに思いを馳せた途端に、文法学習は楽しいものに変わります。
　「過去形は遠い」というイメージをぜひ自分のものにして、文法学習の面白さを味わっていただきたいと思います。

Part 4

The Sochi Olympics: First Japanese male to win the gold medal

ソチ五輪で日本男子初の金メダル

The strategy for the FS is the new "Romeo and Juliet"

After he came to Canada, he realized that there were so many things to be improved upon in his skating such as stamina, techniques and artistry. When he found problems, he tried to solve them by setting a very difficult objective. That was his way of doing things. When practicing his program, he did the "run through" practice repeatedly rather than doing it partially. To maintain enough stamina until the end of the program, he had to divide his energy effectively according to the performance length of the real competitions.

Athletes cannot avoid sickness or injuries. Right after the Four Continents Championships in February, he got the flu. Because of a high fever, he could not practice for 10 days. When he restarted his practice for the World Championships scheduled for the following month, he hurt his left knee. As he had to rest for a week, there was only one week left to practice for the World Championships. Even worse, on the day of his FS at the World Championships, in trying to protect his injured left knee, he sprained his right ankle again, which had been sprained a year earlier. So for the FS on that day, he

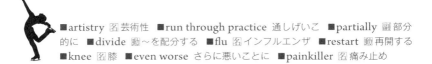

■artistry 图芸術性 ■run through practice 通しげいこ ■partially 副部分的に ■divide 動~を配分する ■flu 图インフルエンザ ■restart 動再開する ■knee 图膝 ■even worse さらに悪いことに ■painkiller 图痛み止め

FS作戦は、新しい『ロミオとジュリエット』で

　カナダに来てから結弦は、体力、技術、芸術性……と自分のスケーティングにはまだまだたくさんの課題があることにあらためて気づいた。課題を見つけると、あえて難しい目標を課すことで克服しようとするのが彼の流儀だった。試合に向けたプログラムの練習でも、部分的な演技の練習ではなく、プログラム演技のすべてを「通し」で演習する「ラン・スルー」を繰り返した。終盤でのスタミナ切れを克服するには、本番の時間を想定して力を配分できるようにしなくてはならない。

　しかし、それでも克服できないのは病気やケガだ。2月の四大陸選手権の直後にはインフルエンザに感染して、高熱のために10日もリンクに立てなかった。翌月の世界選手権に間に合わせようと再開した練習で、今度は左膝を痛めてしまった。1週間休んだために、世界選手権向けの練習は1週間しかなかった。さらに世界選手権のFS当日には、痛めた左膝をかばったことで1年前に痛めた右足首をまたねん挫してしまった。だからあの日のFSは痛み止めを服用しての演技だった。「日本人男子3人でソチに行くためには棄権できない」との意地だった。その後、日本

had to take painkillers to be able to perform. He was determined to go to Sochi with the other two Japanese, and withdrawal was not an option for him. He went for a detailed examination later in Japan. His left knee was diagnosed as having patellar tendinitis, also known as "jumper's knee" due to the overuse of the knee, and the sprained right ankle was judged as chronic. Yuzuru was relieved to know that the injuries were not something serious, but decided to withdraw from the World Team Trophy in April.

Even though he was not able to go on the rink for a month and a half, he kept his positive attitude.

"No athlete can avoid injuries. This is a reminder not to hurt myself more severely. It means that I have to train my body as a whole concentrating on core strengthening. Besides, through my experience this time, now I know how I feel when I have to compete with injuries," he said.

His mind was already moving on to the 2013–2014 season and the planning for the Sochi Olympics.

He had some ideas. He wanted to raise the difficulty level of his SP "Parisienne Walkways." He could show his masculinity with the song, and had scored record points twice before with this song. But he was confident that he could improve the performance further by adding more depth to his interpretation.

■withdrawal 图棄権 ■detailed examination 精密検査 ■be diagnosed as ～と診断される ■patellar tendinitis 膝蓋腱炎 ■chronic 形慢性の ■attitude 图（物事に対する）考え方 ■severely 副ひどく ■masculinity 图男らしさ ■depth 图深さ ■interpretation 图演技

で精密検査を受けると、左膝は酷使(オーバー・ユース)による膝蓋腱炎、いわゆる「ジャンパー膝」。右足首のねん挫は慢性的なものと判定された。悪性なものでなかったことに安堵したが、4月の国別対抗戦は欠場することにした。

　1ヵ月半もの間リンクには上がれなかったが、結弦はあくまでポジティブだった。
　「アスリートにケガはつきもの。これはもっと大きなケガをしないようにという忠告です。五輪にむけて体幹を中心に全身をバランス良く鍛えておきなさいということです。それに今度の経験から、ケガをしながら試合に臨むとどんな心理状態になるかもわかりました」
　「それよりも……」と、心は2013-2014シーズン、ソチ五輪シーズンに向けたプランのことに向かって行った。

　結弦なりに考えていたことがあった。まずSPで演じてきた『パリの散歩道』を、もっと完成度を高めたものにしたかったのだ。大人の男らしさを見せられる曲だったし、2度まで歴代最高得点を出している。しかし、まだ深い演技にする自信があった。それにSPを同じものにしておけば、その分FSでの練習に集中で

And if he did the same SP, he could concentrate on practicing the FS. The previous season, he had been performing "Notre-Dame de Paris." Because of its profound and complicated content, the best approach had been to learn the program components. But would this program be good enough for the Olympics? Some people say that well-known, orthodox music is more likely to be accepted at the Olympics than unfamiliar pieces. Yuzuru thought about using "Romeo and Juliet," which he had used at the World Championships before. It was the tune from the movie starring Leonardo DiCaprio. But as "Romeo and Juliet" is a classic, it has been the subject of movies and musicals many times. The most popular one was a 1968 British–Italian film with Olivia Hussey as Juliet and music by Nino Rota. This famous film music is often still played as a classic. Yuzuru decided on this version of the song.

Yuruzu wrote a letter to Wilson, his choreographer, explaining what he felt about this song. Later, Wilson revealed the content of this "very moving letter" written by Yuzuru.

He wrote, "Please help me. I will do anything to become an Olympic champion. I could die for it. I don't want to wait until 2018. I really want to win now. I'll do anything that you tell me to do. I beg you."

Wilson was the most wanted choreographer. After Yuna, he choreographed for Chan and Fernandez. In the past, Yuzuru had

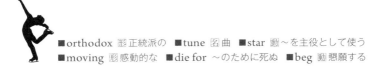

■orthodox 形 正統派の ■tune 名 曲 ■star 動 〜を主役として使う
■moving 形 感動的な ■die for 〜のために死ぬ ■beg 動 懇願する

きる。そのFSは、昨シーズンは『ノートルダム・ド・パリ』でやってきた。重厚で複雑な内容は演技構成力をつけるのには効果的だったが、五輪では果たしてどうだろう？　五輪ではよく知られたオーソドックスな"王道"の曲が受けやすいとも聞く。結弦が想い出したのは、それ以前の世界選手権まで使っていた『ロミオ＋ジュリエット』だった。それは、1996年にレオナルド・ディカプリオが演じた映画の楽曲だった。だが、古典である『ロミオとジュリエット』は、過去に何度も映画やミュージカルになっている。中でも人気があったのは、イギリスとイタリアの合作で、ジュリエットをオリビア・ハッセーが演じ、ニノ・ロータが作曲した1968年版のものだ。その曲は映画音楽の名曲として未だに演奏される。やるならこの曲だ。

　結弦は、この気持ちを振付師のウィルソンに手紙で伝えた。後にウィルソンが、受け取った「とても感動的な手紙」が、こんな内容だったと明かしている。
　「お願いですから手を貸してください。五輪チャンピオンになるためには何でもします。死んだっていいんです。2018年まで待ちたくない。今、どうしても取りたいんです。あなたが教えてくれることは何でもします。助けてください」
　何しろ当代一番の売れっ子振付師、ヨナの後、チャンやフェルナンデスの振付けもしている。『ノートルダム』の時も、結弦

wanted to use "The Phantom of the Opera," but he had to use "Notre-Dame" instead because Wilson would not allow him to do so. "Patrick (Chan) will use it" he had said. Although Yuzuru's English was not that good, he used the strategy of writing a letter to this big shot to express his sincere feelings and to persuade him. Wilson's answer was, "OK. Let's do it!"

For the new FS song, they had to change the sequence of jumps accordingly. They decided to use a quadruple Salchow and toe loop to start the program. In the second half of the program where the scores are 1.1 times more than in the first half, it was determined that the jump sequence would be a triple axel, double toe loop, and triple Lutz, triple Salchow combination. They figured that it would make the base value 74.72, and more points could be expected from the GOE (grade of execution).

〔15〕 Can't beat Patrick Chan?

In July 2013 (seven months before the Sochi Olympics), Yuzuru entered into an affiliation contract with All Nippon Airways (ANA), where ANA would pay his expenses, for example, for travel between Canada and Japan, and also to other countries where competitions were held. It is said that, for a world-class top figure

■big shot 大物　■persuade 動説き伏せる　■accordingly 副それに応じて
■figure 動計算する　■base value 基礎点　■execution 名できばえ
■affiliation 名所属　■expense 名費用　■estimated cost 推定費用

は『オペラ座の怪人』を希望したものの、「それはパトリック（チャン）に使うから」と断られた経緯がある。結弦は、この大物を説得するために、上手でないが心をこめた手紙で口説く作戦を取ったのだ。結果は「OK、それで行こう！」

FSの曲が一新されるとなればジャンプ構成も変わって来る。冒頭の４回転サルコウ、同トゥ・ループの順にして、得点が1.1倍になる後半は、３回転アクセルに２回転トゥ・ループ、３回転ルッツには３回転サルコウをつけるコンビネーション・ジャンプという構成にした。これで基礎点は74.72になり、GOE（できばえ点）の加算も期待できる。

パトリック・チャンには勝てないのか？

翌年２月のソチ五輪が７ヵ月後に迫った７月、結弦は、全日本空輸（ANA）との所属契約を結んだ。カナダと日本との往復や世界各地での試合のための渡航費用などをANAが負担してくれることになった。世界トップクラスの選手ともなれば、年間1300万円は経費がかかるといわれているが、渡航費用の負担も

skater, the estimated cost of competing is about 13 million yen per year. And the financial burden of travel expenses is very heavy. For Yuzuru's "ordinary" family, this support from ANA was a great help. At the press conference, Yuzuru said that he was very happy about it.

At the Finlandia Trophy on October 5 and 6, Yuzuru defeated Artur Gachinski, a very strong rival from Russia, and won the gold medal. The next competition was the second GP Series in Canada on October 25 and 26. In the GP Series, the medalists are scheduled to appear in different competitions to avoid the concentration of high-ranking skaters in one competition. Yuzuru was ranked fourth last season, and he was scheduled to compete with Patrick Chan at this event. Chan was Yuzuru's rival. At the World Championships, his score had exceeded Yuzuru's record high score in the NHK Trophy competition.

At the Cup of Russia in 2010, Yuzuru tried to follow him at the official practice, but he was amazed how fast Chan could skate. Seeing Chan's big quadruple toe loop jump right after Chan had been skating so hard, Yuzuru felt overwhelmed. Since then, he had been strongly aware that he could not become number one in the world without beating Chan. Before this competition, Yuzuru was saying that he would like to beat Patrick. But because he thought about it too much, his result was not great.

■burden 図負担 ■press conference 記者会見 ■exceed 動上回る
■amazed 形驚いた ■overwhelmed 形圧倒された

大きい。これは“普通”の家庭だった羽生家にとっても助かる。結弦も記者会見で「とてもうれしい」と語った。

　10月5、6日のフィンランディア杯では、ロシアの強敵アルトゥール・ガチンスキーを破って優勝。同月25、26日のGPシリーズ第2戦スケートカナダに臨んだ。GPシリーズでは強い出場者が同じ試合に偏らないように、メダリストは別々の大会に出るように組まれる。だが、昨シーズンランクが4位だった結弦は、この大会でパトリック・チャンと対決することになった。結弦のNHK杯での得点記録を世界選手権で抜いているライバルだ。

　2010年のロシア杯の時、公式練習では、チャンの後を追いかけるように滑ってみたが、スピードの差に驚き、そのまま大きな4回転トゥ・ループをするのを見て圧倒された。以来、「チャンに勝てなければ、世界のトップに立てない」と強く意識してきた。この時も、試合の前に「パトリックに勝ちたい！」と語っていたが、意識しすぎは良い結果にならない。

In the SP, his Lutz was not successful. In the FS, he fell on the quadruple jump, and he could rotate only halfway in the triple axel in the second half of the program. His strategy to "build up the base value" was not working, and worse, he finished second with a score 30 points lower than Chan's. He knew the cause of the defeat well, of course.

In November, at the Trophée Éric Bompard (Trophée de France), the fifth GP Series, Yuzuru met Chan again. As Yuzuru had learned his lesson, he did not think about Chan too much and was relaxed before the competition. Chan performed the SP before him and scored 98.52, which was an improvement of his own record. But Yuzuru was observing Chan calmly. And he was talking to reporters about the reason why his program components score could get high points.

"Because all my movements are connected with accurate and complicated footwork I can use my knees and ankles very well and put my weight on my skates. When I do that, I can control my speed freely. So all my steps, skating before jumps and connecting movements can change into various movements. I think that is why my program components will get a high score," he said.

In the FS, he tried to keep his concentration. He fell on two quadruple jumps, but was able to recover from them right away in the latter half of the program like Daisuke Takahashi could.

■build up 〜を積み上げて高める　■observe 動 観察する　■recover from 〜から立ち直る

SPではルッツが決まらない。FSでも4回転で転倒、後半の3回転アクセルが半分しか回れなかった。「基礎点を積み上げれば勝てる」というあの計算はむなしくなり、逆に30点も差を付けられての2位に終わった。もちろん、結弦は自分の敗因をわかっていた。

　11月は、GP第5戦のエリック・ボンパール杯（フランス杯）。今度もチャンと顔合わせした。前回の反省を生かして、チャンを意識しないようにしリラックスして臨んだ。SPでは自分の前にチャンが滑り、98.52点と自己記録を更新したが、結弦はチャンを冷静に観察した。彼は記者たちを前にして、自分の演技構成点が高く評価される理由を語っていた。

　「すべての動きが正確で複雑なフットワークで繋がっているからです。膝と足首をしっかり使って、体重をスケート靴に乗せる。そうすればスピードの緩急が出せるので、ステップもジャンプの助走も、つなぎの演技も多彩な動きに変わる。それが高く評価されていると思います」

　FSでは、集中力を切らせないことを心がけた。4回転2本をミスしたが、高橋大輔のようにすぐに後半をリカバリーできた。だが、チャンはFSでもパーフェクトな演技をして優勝。前回同

But Chan performed perfectly in his FS and won the competition. Like the previous time, there was more than a 30 points difference between Chan and Yuzuru. "I don't know what to do to beat Patrick," he said.

Named in Japan's team for the Olympics by a personal best record

In the athletics world, there is a term called "peaking." It means to train one's body and mental condition so that it is at its best (peak) for the most important competition. Through his many experiences, Yuzuru had become good at it. The audience could see it at the Grand Prix Final in Fukuoka on December 5 and 6. It was the third competition with Chan.

In the previous year, Yuzuru had finished second at the GP Final in Sochi, Russia, held at the venue that would be used for the Sochi Olympics. This time, as it was an important competition before the Olympics starting in two months' time, the organizers were nervous as well. But Yuzuru was able to forget about the second GP Series in which he had been defeated by Chan, and kept his cool.

■peaking 图 ピーキング《本番に向けて心身のコンディションが最高の状態になるように調整すること》 ■peak 图 頂点 ■organizer 图 運営者 ■nervous 形 緊張した

様に30点以上の差をつけられた。「パトリックにはなす術がない」(結弦)

自己ベスト記録でつかみ取った五輪出場

　アスリートの世界には「ピーキング」という言葉がある。一番大事な試合の時に、最高の力が発揮できるように、その日に合わせて心身のコンディションを整えるようにトレーニングすることをいう。結弦は、試合経験を重ねるうちに、このピーキングが上手にできるようになっていた。そう思わせてくれたのが、12月5、6日のGPファイナル福岡大会だった。3度目のチャンとの組合せになった。

　昨年、ロシア・ソチの五輪予定会場で行われたGPファイナルでは、高橋に次ぐ2位だった。今回は、五輪まで2ヵ月の大きな試合であり、運営関係者たちも緊張していた。だが、結弦は、チャンに抑え込まれたGP2戦とは気持ちを切り替えて冷静になることができた。

In his SP "Parisienne Walkways," his jumps, spins and steps were perfect. As it was held in Japan, the venue was packed with fans, and they were cheering for him. Stuffed "Winnie the Poohs," which had become famous as Yuzuru's mascot, and bunches of flowers wrapped tightly so that they would not scatter on the ice, were thrown on the rink one after another. The flower girls could not keep up in retrieving them. In the so-called "Kiss and Cry" waiting area, Coach Orser and Yuzuru waited for his marks to be announced. The score was 99.84. Orser shouted and stood up, then hugged Yuzuru tightly. It was the world record and higher than the 98.52 of Chan's score at the GP in France three weeks earlier. Also, Yuzuru's program components score was higher than Chan's for the first time.

On the following day, Yuzuru performed his FS. He fell on the quadruple jumps in the beginning, but succeeded in the other seven jumps until the second half of the program. When he finished, as he had spent all his energy, he kept his hands on the ice and could not stand up. His score was 193.41 (total 293.25). He had beaten his own best score and it was higher than Chan's score again. It was his dearest wish to win the GP Final. The following day was his 19th birthday, and he celebrated his birthday by this achievement.

■stuffed 形ぬいぐるみの ■bunch 名束 ■scatter 動散らばる ■keep up 〜 し続ける ■so-called 形いわゆる ■mark 名得点 ■one's dearest wish 念願

SP『パリの散歩道』はジャンプもスピンもステップも完璧だった。国内だけあって超満員のファンの声援も大きく、結弦のマスコットとして知られるようになった「クマのプーさん」のぬいぐるみや、花びらが散らばらないようにラッピングされた花束が、次々とリンクに投げ入れられる。フラワーガールたちの回収が追い付かないぐらいだった。待機場所の「キス＆クライ」コーナーで、オーサー・コーチと結果を待つ結弦。発表された得点は99.84。オーサーは「ウォーッ」と立ち上がって結弦を強くハグした。チャンが3週間前のGPフランスで出した98.52を上回る世界記録だった。しかも演技構成点で初めてチャンを上回った。

　翌日のFS。出だしの4回転は転倒したものの、後半まで7つのジャンプは成功。最後のスピンではよろけながらだった。持てるエネルギーのすべてを出し切ってフィニッシュした時は、氷上に手をついたまま立ち上がれなかった。得点193.41（総合293.25）の自己ベストで、やはりチャンを上回った。念願だったGPファイナルに優勝できた翌日は19歳の誕生日。自分から祝福することになった。

He was gradually reaching his peak. Sixteen days after this GP Final, the Japan Championships was held at Saitama Super Arena in Saitama. As a country Japan was allowed to have three men's figure skating places at the Sochi Olympics. The skaters who would qualify to go would be determined at this competition. As there were so many excellent skaters, Yuzuru's place was not guaranteed. But he won again, and won big.

His score was above 100 points in the SP, although it was just a national record as this was not one of the ISU Championships. On the following day, his FS score was 194.70. After the competition, it was announced that Hanyu, Machida and Takahashi had been chosen for Team Japan for the Olympics.

"Oh my God!" screamed at the gold medal announcement

It was December, and a rare opportunity for Yuzuru to be able to stay in Japan. He spent the New Year at his home in Sendai. He was able to see his grandparents and cousins for the first time in a long time, and he relaxed a lot and enjoyed the happy gatherings with them. Then he went back to Toronto at the beginning of January, 2014.

■guaranteed 形確定された　■win big 圧勝する　■scream 動叫ぶ　■rare 形珍しい　■cousin 名いとこ　■for the first time in a long time 久しぶりに　■gathering 名集まり

ピーキングは徐々に上り詰めようとしていた。このGPファイナルから16日後、全日本選手権は埼玉の「さいたまスーパー・アリーナ」で開催された。日本はソチ五輪男子フィギュアに3人の出場枠を確保していたが、この試合で、誰がその3人かが決まる。何しろ層が厚いのだから結弦の出場が確定しているわけでない。だが、結果は圧勝の連覇だった。

　SPでは100点を超えた。ただし、ISU公認試合ではないため国内参考記録である。翌日のFSでは194.70。試合後、日本代表選手は、羽生、町田、髙橋の3人と発表された。

金メダル確定に「オーマイ、ガーッ」

　珍しく国内で過ごせた12月だったが、結弦はそのまま留まり、2014年の正月を故郷の仙台の実家で過ごした。久しぶりに祖父母や従兄弟たちも集まっての賑やかで楽しい時間に、大いにくつろいだ。そして「松の内」が明けると共にトロントに帰った。

"People say that the Olympics are special. They also say that an evil spirit lives in the Olympic Games, and unexpected accidents and miracles happen there. But I don't know because I've never been there," he said.

He tried to gain an impression of the Olympics by talking with Shizuka Arakawa, who is also from Sendai and won Japan's first gold medal at the Olympics. He also spoke with Orser, who is a two-time silver medalist at the Olympics. Ever since he had been in the junior level, he kept saying publicly that he would get a gold medal in Sochi and also in PyeongChang in 2018. But nobody had believed it. But finally, when it had come to the point where he was reported to be the most promising candidate to win gold, it just didn't feel real.

"It seems that there are two persons in me: one who thinks calmly that the Olympics is just one of the big competition during the season. Yet another one is excited to be able go to this dream stage that happens only once in four years. What I'd like to do is to give everything I've got at the Olympics," he said.

At the Sochi Olympics, a new team event of the inter-country skating competition had been added, and it was going to be held before the opening ceremony on February 7. Yuzuru was one of the members of the Japanese team, and was scheduled to participate in the men's SP. He arrived in Sochi on February 3. The SP on the

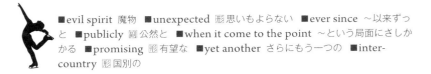

■evil spirit 魔物 ■unexpected 形 思いもよらない ■ever since 〜以来ずっと ■publicly 副 公然と ■when it come to the point 〜という局面にさしかかる ■promising 形 有望な ■yet another さらにもう一つの ■inter-country 形 国別の

The Sochi Olympics: First Japanese male to win the gold medal

「いろんな人が『五輪は特別なものだ』と言う。『五輪には魔物が潜んでいて、思わぬ事故や奇跡が生まれる』とも言うけど、経験のないボクにはよくわからない」

　五輪で日本女子初の金メダリストになった同郷の荒川静香や、2度の五輪で銀メダリストだったコーチのオーサーなどと話して、結弦なりに五輪のイメージをつかもうとした。ジュニアの時から、「ソチで金メダル！　2018年の平昌でも金メダルを取ります」と公言したが、誰にも本気にされなかった。今、本当にその最有力候補と報道されるところに来ても、なかなか実感がわかなかった。

　「シーズン中の大きな大会の一つに過ぎないと考える冷静な自分と、4年に1度しかない夢の舞台に立つと興奮する自分が両方いるようです。考えているのは、限界まで自分の力を出し切りたいということだけです」

　ソチ五輪では初めて国別に競う団体戦の種目が加わり、2月7日の開幕式前日に行なわれることになった。結弦はこれに日本チームとして男子SPに参加することになったために、ソチへは2月3日に入った。6日のSPは良い肩ならし、脚ならしになった。アイドルだった「皇帝」エフゲニー・プルシェンコは、ロシ

6th served as a good opportunity for him to warm up. Yuzuru's hero, "Emperor" Evgeni Plushenko, got Russia's first gold medal at the Olympic Games, and it gave him a total of four Olympic medals. In the past, "the Emperor" had come back from knee and back surgeries three times. But during his pre-program warm-up, he hit his back hard when he landed on the ice, and withdrew from the individual competition. Shortly after, it was announced that he would be retiring from competitive skating. What happens at the Olympics is unpredictable for sure.

In his SP on the 13th, Yuzuru achieved a record high score of 101.45 points. At the FS on the 14th, he was the third person to skate, and he performed "Romeo and Juliet." He fell on the first quadruple Salchow, successfully landed a quadruple toe loop and fell on a triple flip. In the second half of the program, his triple axel and toe loop were successful, but he received a two-point deduction. His feet felt heavy and he could not move well. He wondered if this was the "evil spirit at the Olympics." His combined total score was 280.09, which was lower than his score at the GP Final. He felt that the gold medal was slipping away from him.

But it was Chan who was attacked by "an evil spirit at the Olympics." He made mistakes continuously on his favorite quadruple and triple jumps. His program components score was

■serve as ～としての役割を果たす　■back 名背部　■surgery 名手術　■individual 形個人の　■unpredictable 形予測不可能な　■deduction 名減点　■wonder if ～かどうか不思議に思う　■slip away 逃げ去る

アに最初の金メダルをもたらし、彼自身は、のべ4回の五輪メダリストという記録を作った。だが、膝や椎間板の手術から3度もカムバックしたことのある「皇帝」だったが、13日からの個人戦に向けた練習中に着氷時に腰を強打。演技できずに棄権してしまった。そのまま15日には引退を表明した。まったく五輪は、何が起こるかわからない。

　個人戦に入った13日のSPで、結弦は101.45点という史上最高点を出した。そして14日のFS。結弦は3番目の滑走で『ロミオとジュリエット』を演じた。冒頭の4回転サルコウは転倒、4回転トゥ・ループは成功、3回転フリップで転倒。後半に入っての3回転アクセルやトゥ・ループは決めたが、減点2。脚が重く感じられて体が動かなかった。これも「五輪の魔物」なのか……。総合点はGPファイナルを下回る280.09。金メダルが遠ざかっていくのを感じていた。

　しかし、「五輪の魔物」が襲いかかったのは、次に滑ったチャンの方だった。大得意の4回転でも3回転でもミスが続いた。構成点だけ結弦に勝ったものの技術点では4点以上差がついた。

better than Yuzuru's, but his technical score was more than four points lower than Yuzuru's score. At that moment, the winner of the gold medal was decided. Yuzuru could not watch Chan's performance because he was having an interview at that time. When he heard the result from the reporter, he screamed, "Oh my God! Oh my God! Oh my God!"

He had won the first Olympic gold medal for Japan in the men's figure skating event, following Shizuka Arakawa's gold medal for the women.

I will not write about the series of huge reactions that occurred after Yuzuru received the gold medal on the podium. His serious answers to interviews, the huge welcome at Haneda Airport, the victory parade to hear the cheers of over 90,000 fans, and many other celebration events... I will not mention those either. What I would like to tell you is that Yuzuru was not satisfied with his performance at the Olympics. He was regretful and wanted to perform better at the next competition. "I just want to take my performance to the next level," he thought. He had no intention of taking a break like Chan did.

■huge welcome 大歓迎 ■regretful 形 後悔している ■take ~ to the next level 〜を次の段階に持っていく ■intention 名 〜する意図 ■take a break 休養する

この瞬間、金メダルの行方が決まった。インタビューを受けていて、チャンの試合を見られなかった結弦は、その結果を記者から聞いて、「オーマイ、ガーッ」と3度叫んだ。

　荒川静香に次いで2人目、日本人男子として初のフィギュア金メダリストが誕生した。

　表彰台で金メダルを受けてからの一連の大騒動については省略しよう。生真面目なインタビューでの答えや、羽田での大歓迎、9万人以上に応えた仙台凱旋パレード、たくさんの祝賀行事のことも省きたい。結弦の心の中では、満足した内容ではなかったことの後悔と、その悔いを、次の試合で晴らさなければ納得しないという思いがうずいていた。「もっと高みに持っていきたい」と。チャンのように休養を取るつもりは、みじんもなかった。

❧Column 3❧ Types of spins and steps

Jumps are not the only element of a beautiful figure skating performance. Some of the position techniques like spins and steps are not scored, but are used to connect each element and to create impressive accents through their combination.

(Note: The names in parentheses are the abbreviations. For example, Combination Spin is written as CoSp.)

1. Sitting Spin (SSp): A sitting spin is a spin in which the skater is in a "shoot the duck" position. The free leg (the leg not used for skating) is extended forward, and the buttocks are not higher than the level of the skating knee.

2. Camel Spin (CSp): A camel spin is a spin that uses the skating leg as a pivot while the skater's upper body and free leg are horizontal or in a T-shape to the ice.

3. Layback Spin (LSp): This spin is usually performed by women. Using the skating leg as a pivot, the skater's back is arched and the head is dropped back with the free leg in an attitude position.

4. Donut Spin: A donut spin is a variation of a camel spin. The skater's head is pulled toward the free leg's foot so that the skater's head, torso, and free leg form a donut shape. This requires extreme flexibility in the body.

〔コラム3〕　スピンやステップの種類

　華麗なフィギュアの演技を構成するのはジャンプだけではない。採
点対象にならないポジション技もあるが、演技をつなぎ、印象的なア
クセントとして色々に組み合わせて用いられる。（カッコ内はスピン
の略称。コンビネーション・スピンなどはCoSpなどと書く）

　1. シット・スピン（SSp）：片足で"しゃがんだ姿勢"で回るスピン。
フリーレッグ(軸足に使っていない足)をまっすぐ前に伸ばし、お尻の
下の位置が、膝よりも低くなる。

　2. キャメル・スピン（CSp）：伸ばした片足を軸にして、上体を氷と
平行になるように倒してTの字型になって回る。

　3. レイ・バック・スピン（LSp）：主に女子が行なう。片足を軸に、フ
リーレッグをまっすぐ後ろに伸ばした姿勢で上体を反らした状態で回
る。

　4. ドーナツ・スピン：キャメル・スピンの変形。フリーレッグを後ろ
から頭につけ、ドーナツのように丸く見える。優れた柔軟性が要求さ
れる技。

5. Biellmann Spin: Denise Biellmann performed this spin for the first time in 1981. The blade of the free leg is held with either one or both hands. And the free leg is pulled from behind up and over the head.

6. Ina Bauer: Performed by Ina Bauer in 1950 for the first time, in this spin one foot is on a forward edge and the other is on a backward edge. Both toes are apart at 180 degrees, and the skater glides sideways. Shizuka Arakawa bends over almost completely backward in what is called a layback Ina Bauer.

7. Eagle: This spin is also called the Spread Eagle. The skater extends both arms, spreads the legs 180 degrees, with toes pointing out, and then glides sideways. Both edges make a single tracing on the ice.

8. Butterfly: The skater makes a two-foot, twisting takeoff, and jumps in the air with a body position that is momentarily near-horizontal to the ice.

9. Pivot: One toe is inserted into the ice as a pivot point. The other foot travels around the pivot point and draws a circle.

10. Candle: This spin is also known as a Charlotte. From the camel posture with one leg lifted high in the air, the skater bends forward to the knee. The skater's legs look like a straight stick.

5. **ビールマン・スピン**：1981年にデニス・ビールマン選手が世界で初めて行った。両手あるいは片手でフリーレッグのブレードを持ち、背後から頭上に持ち上げた形のスピン。

6. **イナ・バウアー**：1950年にイナ・バウアーが初めて行った。足を前後に開き、つま先を180度開いて真横に滑る技。荒川静香のは極限まで上半身をそらせるレイ・バック・イナ・バウアー。

7. **イーグル**：スプレッド・イーグルともいう。両手を広げ、両足を伸ばした状態で180度に広げ、つま先を外に向けて開いた状態で横に滑る。左右のエッジの軌跡が重なる。

8. **バタフライ**：氷をけって全身を空中に浮かし、一瞬、氷と平行にする。

9. **ピボット**：片足のトゥを氷について軸として動かさず、もう片方で円を描く。

10. **キャンドル**：シャーロットともいう。高く足を上げたキャメルの姿勢から頭を下に倒して膝に付けるようにし、足を真上に上げた1本の棒のような体勢になる。

覚えておきたい英語表現

I could die for it.（p. 108, 下から6行目）
そのためには死んだっていい。

　この文に使われているcouldはPart3で解説した用法そのものです。比喩として使われていて、本当に死ぬわけではないので「遠い可能性」を示すためにcouldが使われています。

　dieの意味を知らない方は少ないでしょう。とはいえ、意味が意味だけにしっかりと深いレベルまで学ぶ機会が少ないのではないでしょうか？　人は死から逃れることができないのは、洋の東西を問いません。死に関する表現は日本語同様とても多くあります。似た意味を持つ表現と共に学んでみましょう。

　dieは「死ぬ」を表す最も一般的な言葉ですが、日本語の「死ぬ」ほどの強い響きは持っていません。「亡くなる」に近いイメージです。もっと確実に、「亡くなる」と表現したい場合は「pass away」を使うとよいでしょう。

　他に「be dead」という表現もあります。be動詞が必要なことからもわかるようにdeadは形容詞で「死んでいる状態」を表します。be deadは直接的・衝撃的なイメージが先行します。戦争映画などの人が亡くなるシーンで、「He's dead!」のようなセリフが「奴が死んだ！」とか「え？ 死んでる！」という字幕で紹介されることがよくあります。衝撃的で、悼む気持ちがまだ湧きでてこない発言者の気持ちをよく表しています。

　不慮の事故などで亡くなる場合には「be killed」が使われます。dieよりも「被害にあって死んだ」という被害性が強調される表現です。

　他にも「depart（逝く）」、「perish（非業の死を遂げる）」などの固い表現もあります。スラングに近い言葉としては「kick the bucket（くたばる）」があります。

　日本語でも「もう死にそう」とか「〜できたら死んでもいい」というように、死ぬ動作そのものではなく形容的な表現として「死」という言葉を使いますが、英語でも同様です。とてもよく使われるので是非覚えておきましょう。

I would rather die than go to school.
学校に行くくらいなら死んだ方がましだ。

I nearly died when I met my ex-girlfriend at the party.
パーティーで元カノに会って死ぬほど驚いたよ。

I'm dying for a drink.
酒を一杯飲みたくて仕方ない。

I'm dying for hunger.
もうお腹ペコペコ。（お腹が空いて死にそう）

Never say die!
頑張れ！（弱音を吐くな！）

My wrist watch is really something. It is to die for.
私の腕時計はかなりのものだよ。そりゃあ、素晴らしいよ。（「その時計のために死んでもいいくらいだ」の意）

She died laughing.
彼女は大笑いした。

Part 5

*Fighting injuries
and sickness*

ケガ、病気とも闘いながら

🎧19 Collision with a Chinese skater during practice!

In March, after the Sochi Olympics, Yuzuru won the World Championships for the first time at the Saitama Super Arena. During only one season, he won the titles of the GP, Japan Championships, the Olympics and World Championships. But what meant more to him than those titles was the fact that he had been able to finally land cleanly on the quadruple Salchow and toe loop in the one competition, which he had been trying to achieve for so long.

During the off-season, Yuzuru appeared in many ice shows to express gratitude to the people who cheered for him. The majority of the audience were Yuzuru's fans. Every time he finished his program, they threw stuffed Poohs and flowers onto the ice. While the spectacular shows continued, he never forgot the victims of the disaster in Tohoku. He wanted to do something as a skater, and so he donated six million yen, which he had received from the government as a reward for his win at the Sochi Olympics, and the royalties from his photography book to his former home rink. In between the shows, he practiced various quadruple jumps. As he saw many skaters try quadruple jumps, he realized that times had changed and male figure skaters needed quadruple jumps to win.

■collision 名衝突 ■title 名選手権、称号 ■for so long 長い間 ■express gratitude to ～に感謝の意を表明する ■majority 名多数 ■spectacular 形華やかな ■donate 動寄付する ■reward 名報奨金 ■royalty 名印税

練習中に中国の選手と衝突！

　ソチ五輪後、3月に「さいたまスーパー・アリーナ」で開催された世界選手権で、結弦は初めて優勝した。たった1シーズンのうちに、GP王者、全日本王者、そして五輪王者に世界王者のタイトルを手にしたことになる。だが、そのことより、彼にとっての収穫は、この2シーズン、ずっと追いかけてきてできなかったこと、4回転サルコウと4回転トゥ・ループの両方を1試合中に成功できたことだった。

　オフシーズンには、応援してくれた人たちへの感謝も込めてたくさんのアイスショーに出演した。場内に詰めかけた人たちの多くが結弦のファンであり、演技が終わるたびに、氷上を花束と「クマのプーさん」人形が埋めた。華やかなショーが続く間、結弦は東北の被災者のことを忘れなかった。スケーターである自分にできることとして、ソチ五輪優勝で政府からもらった報奨金600万円や、写真集などの出版印税を、かつてのホームリンクに寄付した。また、合間には4回転のさまざまなジャンプの練習もした。五輪でたくさんの選手が4回転に挑むのを見て、男子フィギュアが完全に4回転で勝負する時代に突入したことを確信したからだ。

Then the 2014–2015 season started. He renewed his determination and made a plan for the new season. For the SP, he chose a quiet song, "Ballade No. 1" by Chopin. This was the first piano music he had used. The choreographer was Jeffrey Buttle. For the FS, he selected "The Phantom of the Opera," which he had wanted to use for a long time. It was choreographed by Shae-Lynn Bourne. They put difficult combination jumps into the second half of the program. And they decided to try this new program for the first time at the GP Cup of China held in Shanghai in November.

But an accident happened in Shanghai, during the six-minute FS warm-up at night on November 8.

Yuzuru and Han Yan of China were skating backward at full speed. When they approached the center of the rink and turned around, they collided with each other. Both of them fell on the ice and did not get up. All the practice in the rink was stopped immediately. Yuzuru had blood on his face. Yan seemed to have hit his chin and chest hard. Yuzuru moved to rink side with the help of medical staff, and was dragging his left leg. Orser quickly called the doctor attached to Team U.S.A. Yuzuru's head and chin were heavily dressed with tape to stop the bleeding. Yan received medical treatment from the same staff.

■second half of ～の後半　■approach 動接近する　■turn around 振り向く
■collide with ～と衝突する　■chin 名顎　■drag 動ひきずる　■be dressed
with ～を身に着けて　■bleed 動出血する

そして迎えた2014−2015シーズン。気持ちを新たに今シーズンのプランを決めた。SPは、初めてのピアノ曲でショパンの『バラード第1番』、静かな曲だ。振付けはジェフリー・バトル。FSは前からやりたかった『オペラ座の怪人』で、振付けはシェイ＝リーン・ボーン。難しいジャンプのコンビネーションを後半に盛り込んだ。このプログラムで臨む初戦を、11月上海で開催のGP中国杯にした。

　事故は、その上海で、11月8日夜、FS前に行う6分間練習時に起きた。

　結弦と中国のハン・ヤンが、互いに後ろ向きに猛スピードで滑っており、リンク中央で接近して振り向いた瞬間に激突した。氷上に倒れた二人は起き上がる気配もない。すぐにリンク内すべての練習は中断。結弦は顔から出血していた。ヤンも顎と胸部を強打したようだ。医療スタッフに支えられてリングサイドに移された結弦は左脚をひきずっていた。オーサーは、すぐに米国チームに帯同していたドクターを呼んだ。結弦の頭は止血テープでぐるぐる巻きにされ、顎にも貼られた。ヤンも同じスタッフから治療を受けた。

As a result of the check-up on-site, the diagnosis was that Yuzuru had not hit his head on the ice, and the injury to his chin was just a scratch resulting from the collision. It was not too serious, so the doctor did not order him to stop competing. When asked if he wanted to withdraw, he repeatedly said, "I will skate." Orser nodded to show his approval. If he withdrew, he might not qualify for the GP Final.

Ten minutes later, the six-minute warm-up practice started again. Yuzuru practiced with the tape on his head to stop any bleeding. Yan did not practice, but decided to perform. Yan was born in 1996. He had won at the 2012 World Junior Championships, and placed seventh at the 2014 Sochi Olympics. He was the rising star in China. The accident was nobody's fault, but Yuzuru worried about Yan. Yan came to see Yuzuru before the competition and told him, "Let's do our best."

Yuzuru insisted on skating in the FS, but the results were miserable due to the injuries. But thanks to the good SP score, he finished second overall. Yan performed his whole program and came sixth overall. After the competition, Yuzuru was treated at the medical center. He received three stitches to his head and seven stitches to his chin. He had also hurt his sartorius muscle above the knee and sprained his right foot joint.

■on-site 形その場での　■diagnosis 图診断　■scratch 图擦り傷　■approval 图了承　■insist on 意地でも〜する　■miserable 形悲惨な　■stitch 图（針の）ひと縫い　■sartorius 图縫工筋

その場での診察の結果、頭は氷上に打っていないこと、アゴ
はぶつけた擦り傷と診断された。ドクター・ストップをかけるほ
どではなかった。棄権するかどうかを聞かれた結弦は、「ボクは
滑ります」と繰り返し、オーサーも了承の意味でうなずいた。出
なければGPファイナルへの出場が危うくなるからだった。

　10分後に再開された6分間練習のリンクに、結弦は頭に止血
テープを巻いた状態で立った。ヤンは、練習を止めたが、本番
には出るという。1996年生まれの彼は、2012年世界ジュニアで
優勝し、2014年ソチオリンピックにも出場して7位になった。
中国若手の期待の星だ。この事故は、どちらが悪いというので
もなかったが、結弦はヤンを気遣った。本番前にはヤンから結
弦のところに来て、「お互いにがんばろう」と声をかけた。

　意地で滑ったFSだが、ケガの影響で内容はボロボロ。SPの
得点に助けられて総合2位。ヤンも最後まで滑り切って総合6
位に入賞した。試合後、結弦は医務室で治療を受け、頭を3針、
顎を7針縫った。左膝上の縫工筋も挫傷、右足関節もねん挫し
ていた。

Competing with a stomachache of unknown cause, then an operation

On November 28, twenty days after the injury in Shanghai, Yuzuru was standing in the rink for the NHK Trophy which was the sixth and the last GP Series of the season. He performed despite the pain in his left leg, and placed fourth following Daisuke Murakami, Sergei Voronov and Takahito Mura. He narrowly qualified for the GP Final as the sixth skater. At the interview after the competition, he spoke more than usual. Or, he was talking and thinking at the same time as if he were doing some soul-searching.

"I don't wish I could go back to the condition I was in before the Cup of China (when I was injured). The word 'back' has negative meaning for me. The mistakes I made at the NHK Trophy are a minus now, but they will become a plus next time. Rather, I'm thankful for the opportunity to face many walls to climb up, and I'm really enjoying it. Being weak means that there is a possibility to become strong. After I climb up these walls, I'm sure I will be able to see beautiful scenery beyond them," he said.

■unknown 形不明の　■narrowly 副ぎりぎりで　■soul-searching 名自己分析　■go back to ～に戻る　■thankful for ～をありがたく思う　■face 動～に立ち向かう　■scenery 名景色

原因不明の腹痛を抱えての参戦、そして手術

　上海でのケガから20日後の11月28日、結弦はGPシリーズ最終6戦であるNHK杯のリンクに立っていた。左脚の痛みを抱えたままの演技で、村上大介やセルゲイ・ボロノフ、無良崇人にメダルを奪われての4位。ぎりぎりの6番目でGPファイナル出場資格を手に入れた。試合後のインタビューで、結弦はいつもよりたくさん話をした。というより、話しながら考えをまとめ、自分で自分の心を探るように話し続けた。

　「（ケガをした）中国杯の前に戻れたらとは思いません。"戻す"という言葉は自分にとってマイナス。NHK杯でのミスは、今はマイナスでも、次に向けてのプラスになるものです。むしろたくさん乗り越える壁を作っていただいて、こんなに楽しいことはない。自分が弱いということは強くなれる可能性があるということ。この壁を超えた先にある景色は絶対に良いものだと思っています」

Yuzuru's positive mentality is beyond that of an ordinary person. No matter how bad the mistakes are, he raises the bar higher and higher and motivates himself. This "positive thinking" is his way of life. And he actually lives that way. That is what sets him apart from ordinary people. His records after the NHK Trophy proves that. In December in Barcelona, he won the GP Final for two years in a row, and became the first Japanese male skater to do so. But bad things happened to him after that when nobody was expecting it.

After returning from the GP Final in Barcelona, he started to suffer from a stomachache the cause of which was unknown. When he pushed out or pulled in his stomach, it hurt badly. Soon, the part of the stomach below the navel became swollen to about the size of a table tennis ball. As the pain was so severe, he went to see a doctor. He was diagnosed with a bladder problem related to the urachus. They decided not to do the operation right away. But after he came back to his home in Sendai, the swollen part ruptured, and blood and pus gushed out. The doctor suggested operating immediately, but he just had first aid with some gauze and tape so he could take part in the Japan Championships on the 26th. At the Japan Championships in Nagano, he competed with the gauze and tape under his costume, and won three times in a row. Only a few people knew about Yuzuru's condition at that time.

■no matter how どんなに～であろうとも　■apart from　～から離れて ■prove 動証明する　■navel 名へそ　■swollen 形腫れた　■bladder 名膀胱 ■urachus 名尿膜管　■rupture 動破裂する　■pus 名膿　■gush out 噴き出す　■take part in　～に出場する

あくまでポジティブに考える結弦の精神力は、ちょっと常人離れしている。どんなに失敗しても「先へ、上へ」と目標を掲げ続け、モチベーションを高める彼の「心の流儀」は、完全に彼の生き方になっている。そして実践して見せるところが、さらに常人離れしている。その後の戦績がそれを示している。12月バルセロナで開催のGPファイナルは、日本人男子初の2連覇。同月の長野での全日本選手権は3連覇。だが、この間に別の不運がとりついていたことに気づく人はいなかった。

　バルセロナのGPファイナルを終えて帰国する時から、原因不明の腹痛に苦しんでいた。押したり引っ張ると重く痛む。やがてへその下がピンポン玉みたいに腫れる。痛みに耐えかねて診察を受けた結果、「尿膜管遺残症」と診断されたが、様子をみることにした。だが、仙台の自宅に帰ると腫れた部分が破裂して血と膿が噴き出した。病院では「すぐに手術を」と言われたが、26日には全日本選手権があるからとガーゼとテープで応急処置してもらった。長野での全日本選手権は、コスチュームの下にガーゼとテーピングをして戦い、3連覇したことになる。周囲でこの間の事情を知る人はほとんどいなかった。

He could finally have surgery on December 30. He had a four-centimeter cut on his abdomen. The doctor ordered him to be hospitalized for two weeks and to rest for a month. The condition had started before his birth but it gave rise to clinical problems when Yuzuru was 20. "I thought that beyond one wall, there might be another wall," he said.

Sprained ankle due to avoiding use of operated area

In 2015, Yuzuru spent the New Year in hospital. Then, he rested at home and restarted practice in February. It was now less than two months until the World Championships in Shanghai in March. During the operation, his fascia was cut, and he worried about it. He was concerned about his weakened muscle strength after the hospitalization and rest. They say, "If you don't skate one day, it will take three days to get back to normal." Yuzuru's anxiousness was understandable. He cut short his rest to three weeks, and started practicing quadruple jumps. But when he landed on a toe loop, he sprained his right ankle this time. So again, he had to rest, this time for two weeks.

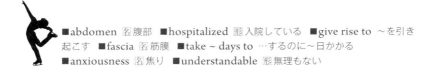

■abdomen 名腹部 ■hospitalized 形入院している ■give rise to ～を引き起こす ■fascia 名筋膜 ■take ~ days to …するのに～日かかる ■anxiousness 名焦り ■understandable 形無理もない

ちゃんと手術してもらったのは12月30日。腹部を4cm切り、医師からは、2週間の入院と1ヵ月の安静を厳命された。この病気は、胎児期に臍と膀胱をつないでいた尿膜管が体内に残っていたために化膿したものだが、それがちょうど20歳の大人になった時に発症したことになる。「壁の先には、やっぱり壁しかないのかと思いました」(結弦)

手術した患部を、無意識にかばってねん挫

　2015年の正月は病院で迎え、自宅療養して、練習を再開したのは2月に入ってからだった。3月下旬に上海で開催される世界選手権までは2ヵ月弱しかない。腹部の筋膜を切る手術だったことや、入院・安静中に落ちた筋力のことが気になってしかたなかった。何しろ「1日滑らなかったら、調子を戻すのに3日かかる」と言われている。結弦が焦るのも無理はない。安静を3週間できりあげて、4回転の練習に入ったが、トゥ・ループの着氷時に、今度は右足首をねん挫してしまった。またもや2週間の休養となった。

"I wasn't aware of it, but my body seemed to be protecting the operated area. As my muscles have become atrophic, I can't fully rotate my body. The inside and outside of my ankle is swollen so badly, I can't wear shoes anymore," he said.

As he could not practice, he spent his time watching his own performance on the video repeatedly, talking to his family and writing e-mails to coach Orser in Toronto to ask for his advice. That situation left him only four weeks to practice for Shanghai.

The World Championships was held at the Shanghai Oriental Sports Center where Yuzuru had had the collision five months earlier. The SP started on March 27. Although he landed low on a quadruple toe loop and put both hands down at the start, he performed the rest of the elements beautifully and placed first. On the following day, in the FS, his two quadruple jumps were not successful, but he performed well in the second half of the program and came third. Overall, Javier Fernandez won the title, which was the first time a Spanish skater had done so, Yuzuru won the silver medal and Denis Ten got the bronze. These same three skaters had scored high at the Sochi Olympics as well.

■not aware of ～に無意識で ■atrophic 形 萎縮した ■put both hands down 両手をつく ■rest of ～の残り

「無意識に身体が患部をかばうんですね。筋肉が萎縮して回転しきれない。足首の内側も外側もパンパンに腫れて、靴に足が入らない状態になりました」

　もう練習すらできない状態の中で、結弦は、自分の演技のビデオを繰り返し見たり、家族と話したり、トロントにいるコーチのオーサーにメールで相談するなどして過ごした。だから、上海に向けての練習は4週間弱しかなかった。

　約5ヵ月前の激突が想い出される「上海東方体育中心」（The Shanghai Oriental Sports Center）での世界選手権大会は、3月27日にSPが始まった。冒頭の4回転トゥ・ループは低い位置で着氷してしまって両手をついたが、残りのエレメンツはきれいに決めて1位。翌日のFSは、2つの4回転が成功しなかったものの後半を踏みとどまって3位。総合では、ハビエル・フェルナンデスがスペイン人初の優勝、結弦が銀メダル、デニス・テンが銅メダルを獲得した。この顔ぶれはソチ五輪の時と同じである。

"I really felt frustrated when I lost. So while I was congratulating Javier, I started to cry. When I win, Javier gives me his sincere blessing... I'm not making an excuse but I performed the SP and FS without any mistakes many times when I was practicing a week before the competition. My peak came too early and I was not at my best on the day of my performance. I guess there are many things that I could learn from my mistakes," he said.

At the end, Yuzuru said that he owed his positive character to his parents. He went back to the hotel, where his mother was waiting for him. He placed the silver medal around her neck as he has always done since he was a child.

■congratulate 動～におめでとうを言う　■bless 動～を祝福する　■make an excuse 言い訳をする　■owe 動～のおかげである

「悔しかったのでハビエルに『おめでとう』と言いながら泣いてしまった。自分が優勝した時は、ハビエルが心から祝福してくれるのに……。言い訳ではないですが、試合の1週間前の練習ではSPもFSも何度もノーミスでできたんです。ピーキングが早すぎて、少し調子が落ちたところに本番が来てしまった。失敗しないと気づけないことはたくさんあります」

　最後に、このポジティブな性格は「両親からもらったもの」と語った結弦は、ホテルに帰ると、中国まで同行してくれた母の首に銀色のメダルをかけた。感謝の気持ちを込めて、子供の頃から続けている結弦の習慣である。

覚えておきたい英語表現

That is what sets him apart from ordinary people. (p. 144, 4行目)
それこそが彼を通常の人からかけ離れた存在にしているものなのだ。

That is what〜（That's what〜）で「それこそまさしく〜だ」と、that以下を強調する表現です。日常生活で使うと、自然に会話を彩ることができます。
　例えば、10代の女の子がスイーツの話題で盛り上がっている様子を見て……

　　　　That's what teenage girls do(are).　　10代の女の子ってああだよね。

　いくつになっても、細々と世話を焼きたがったり口を挟んでくる母親にうんざりしている友達に……

　　　　That's what moms do(are).　　　　母親ってそんなもんだよ。

動詞のcallを加えて、以下のような表現に発展させることもできます。

　　　　Oh, that's what I call rock'n'roll.　　これこそが本物のロックだよ！

疑問文に変えて、驚きや呆れた気持ちを表現することもあります。

　　　　A: Have you checked their new rock'n'roll number?
　　　　B: Oh, come on, is that what you call it?
　　　　A: 彼らの新しいロックナンバー（曲）を聞いたかい？
　　　　B: おいおい、頼むよ、あんなのがロックだというのかい？

> I guess there are many things that I could learn from my mistakes.
> (p. 150, 6行目)
>
> 失敗から学べることはたくさんあると思う。

guessは「～だと推測する」という意味です。元々の意味が「推測する」なので、「I guess ～」は話す内容が不確かなことや、話し手が躊躇しながら話す際に、「～だと思うよ」と個人の判断を述べるときに使われます。

    I guess he didn't have time to read your mail.
    彼は君のメールを読む時間がなかったんじゃないかなあ。

    I guess I'm not hungry any more.
    （自分が）もう空腹ではないように思えるねえ。→遠慮がちに食事の勧めを断る表現

    A: Are you O.K.?   ちょっと大丈夫？
    B: Yes, I guess so.   うん、大丈夫だと思う。

guessに似た使い方をする単語にsupposeもあります。

また、guessにはGuess what!「ねえちょっと聞いてよ！」という慣用的表現もあります。ドラマなどでよく聞く表現です。

Part 6

Beating his own world record

自己の世界新記録を更新

"Seimei" inspired by the film "Onmyoji"

Yuzuru participated in the World Team Trophy and several ice shows, and came back to his base city Toronto in late April. He had to prepare for the 2015–2016 season starting in the summer of 2015. In May, he started to make a plan by thinking about the music and elements of his performance as usual.

For the SP, he had already decided to use Chopin's "Ballade No. 1" again. It was rather easy to perform songs used in operas and musicals because the songs themselves had a story to tell. But with this quiet piano music, it was difficult to express emotions in the performance. He had been performing this program for a year now, but he never finished it without any mistakes. In order to achieve a flawless performance, he had to consolidate his delicate sensitivity as an artist and his solid techniques as an athlete. Yuzuru wanted to challenge that bar again and hoped to beat his own SP world record, which he had kept for two seasons, through his own ability.

■inspired by ～に触発される　■flawless 形非の打ちどころがない
■consolidate 動統一する　■bar 名（走り高跳びの）バー、高い目標

映画『陰陽師』に触発された『SEIMEI』

　結弦が、国別対抗戦やいくつかのアイスショーをこなしてから本拠地のトロントに戻ったのは、4月下旬のことだった。2015年夏からスタートする2015−2016シーズンに備えなくてはならない。5月からのプラン作りは、例によって曲や演技の構成を考えるところから始まった。

　SPについては、ショパンの『バラード第1番』を継続すると決めていた。このピアノだけの静かなクラシック曲は、オペラやミュージカルで使われるストーリー性のある曲と違って感情移入した表現が難しい。1年やってみたがノーミスで演じきれたこともない。アーチストとしてのデリケートな感性とアスリートとしての確実な技術を統一しなくてはならない。結弦は、その高みにもう一度挑戦して、自分が2シーズン保持しているSPの世界記録を自身の力で超えてみたかった。

For the FS, Yuzuru insisted on changing the music to the theme song from a 2001 Japanese film, "Onmyoji." An English version of this film had been released as well. "Onmyoji" actually existed in Japan in the Heian period (between 794 and 1185). Their court responsibilities were to divine good and bad fortune for dates and places and offer prayers. Mansai Nomura, a kyogen performer, played the starring role of Seimei Abe in this film, which was based on a fantastic novel written by Baku Yumemakura. The music was composed by Shigeru Umebayashi. Instead of using the name "Onmyoji," Yuzuru named the song "Seimei," taking it from the name of Seimei Abe. He chose Shae-Lynn Bourne for choreography. She had worked on last season's "The Phantom of the Opera" as well. Although this program was based on a Japanese theme, Yuzuru thought it should not be "too Japanese" so that it would be easily accepted by foreign audiences as well. That was the thought behind this choice.

Still, Yuzuru and Bourne watched a lot of recordings of Noh and Kyogen plays, and learned such things from them as how to walk without moving the upper body. He also got advice directly from Mansai Nomura about the symbolic, unique hand gesture before the performance. "He was the best among the many apprentices I have had in the past. I didn't have to say much to him as he could understand my advice instantly," said Nomura about Yuzuru's excellent learning ability.

■exist 動存在する ■court 名宮廷 ■responsibility 名義務 ■divine 動～を占う ■offer prayers 祈祷する ■theme 名テーマ ■apprentice 名弟子

FSは、結弦の意見で、英語版でも公開されている2001年の日本映画『陰陽師』のテーマ曲に変えることにした。平安時代に実在した『陰陽師』は、宮廷に務めて公的行事の日時や場所の吉凶を占い、祈祷も行う役職である。作家・夢枕獏の奇想天外な原作で、主役の安倍晴明を演じたのは狂言師・野村萬斎、作曲は梅林茂だった。結弦はその曲名を『Onmyoji』とせず、主人公の名前から『SEIMEI』とした。振付師は、昨シーズンの『オペラ座の怪人』を手がけてくれたシェイ=リーン・ボーン。日本的な「和」がテーマではあるが、外国人が振付けることで、「日本っぽくし過ぎない」方が海外にもわかりやすいと考えた。

　それでも結弦とボーンは、能や狂言の映像をたくさん見て、上体をぶらさずに歩む動きなどを研究した。演技開始前の独特の印を切るポーズなどは、野村萬斎から直接アドバイスを受けた。その野村は、結弦の理解力の高さを、「今まで教えてきた弟子の中でも一番、打てば響くようだった」と語っている。

In order to best express the world of "Seimei," Yuzuru gave a lot of thought to the costume as well. The design was inspired by "kariginu," which were clothes with arabesque patterns that were worn in the Heian period. They also planned jump sequences that they had thought about but never realized in the previous season; a quadruple Salchow and a quadruple toe loop at the beginning of the performance and consecutive quadruple jumps in the second half of the program.

Rematch with Chan who came back from his break

The first competition of the season in mid-October was the Autumn Classic International held in Barrie (not far from Toronto) in Canada. On October 14, the rotation in the quadruple toe loop was not sufficient in the second half of the SP. Yuzuru had jumped the triple Lutz beautifully during a six-minute warm-up practice, but his pivot was not straight in the performance. On the following day, his quadruple and consecutive jumps were not successful in the FS. But he stayed focused in the latter half of the program and won gold. On October 30 and November 1, he was still feeling frustrated when Skate Canada, the second GP Series, started. Patrick Chan was there after his year-long break. So the fight between these two rivals restarted in this season.

■give a lot of thought to 〜についてよく考える　■rematch 動再度対決する
■sufficient 形足りている　■pivot 名回転軸　■stay focused 気を散らさない

『SEIMEI』の世界を表現するために衣装も工夫した。平安時代の装束である「狩衣」をイメージさせる唐草文様入りにした。ジャンプは、昨シーズンにも計画しながら一度も実現できなかった構成、つまり冒頭に４回転サルコウ、４回転トゥ・ループ、後半に４回転の連続ジャンプにした。

休養から復帰したチャンとの対決再開

　シーズン最初の試合は10月中旬、カナダ・トロントからも近いバリーでの「オータムクラシック」だったが、14日、SP後半の４回転トゥ・ループは回転不足。６分間練習ではきれいに跳んでいた３回転ルッツは軸が傾いた。翌日のFSでも４回転も連続ジャンプもミスした。それでも後半は踏みとどまって優勝。悔しさを引きずったまま、同月30日、11月１日のGPシリーズ第２戦「スケートカナダ」に臨んだ。この試合には、１年間休養していたパトリック・チャンも出てくる。因縁の対決が再開されるシーズンになった。

Yuzuru tried not to pay too much attention to Chan. But when Chan succeeded in the quadruple jumps in the SP, he was distracted after all. His "quadruple in the second half of the program" had been problematic for him, and he failed again at this competition and finished the program with a score of 73.25. It was almost 30 points lower than his best score. "Chan's existence had nothing to do with my performance. I was thinking too much about not making mistakes," he said. On the following day, he shifted his mood, and successfully landed two quadruple jumps at the start, which was exactly what he had been practicing. But overall, Chan claimed the title and Yuzuru won the silver medal.

He was six points behind Chan in the program components score even after performing "Seimei" wholeheartedly. But he still felt confident.

"Patrick's strength is his ability to control his power well and finish the performance cleanly. My program "Seimei" will get better. It's just that I still haven't been able to digest the music well enough. From now until the NHK Trophy, I will work my guts out for the next three weeks," he said.

■problematic 形問題のある　■nothing to do with ～とは関係がない　■shift one's mood 気持ちを切り替える　■claim the title 優勝する　■digest 動体得する　■work one's guts out 多大な努力をする

意識しないようにと思っても、自分の前のチャンがSPで4回転を決めれば、どうしても注意散漫になる。課題にしてきた「後半の4回転」をまたもミスして、結弦の得点は73.25。自己ベストより30点近くも低かった。本人は、「チャンは関係ない。〝ノーミスで〟という意識にとらわれ過ぎた」と答えた。意識を切り替えた翌日のFSでは、冒頭の4回転2本を決めて、練習通りの成果を出した。総合結果は、復帰したチャンに負けての銀メダルだった。

　想いを込めて取り組んだ『SEIMEI』の演技構成点でも6点差がついた。だが、強気だった。

　「パトリックの強さは自分の力を上手に加減して、演技をクリーンに仕上げる力。『SEIMEI』は、まだまだ伸ばせるプログラムで、曲をまだ自分のものにできていないだけ。これからNHK杯までの3週間、血のにじむような努力をして見せます」

He "worked his guts out" mainly on the two quadruple jumps in the SP. One was a "quadruple toe loop–triple toe loop" combination. According to the rules, only a "quadruple axel" or a "quadruple jump taking off from a difficult approach" could be included in a program. The quadruple axel was extremely difficult and nobody had been successful yet. But a "quadruple jump taking off from a difficult approach" might be possible for Yuzuru. He practiced hard so that he could jump a "quadruple Salchow" using the "eagle" as an entrance. The eagle in classical ballet is a position where the toes are turned out to the sides 180 degrees and the arms are spread straight like an eagle's wings. Because the body faces sideways in the eagle position, it is very difficult to take off without steps. And to jump high enough for a quadruple jump from the eagle is much more difficult. But Yuzuru had a strong feeling that he could pull it off.

Surpasses a total score of 300, and claims to be an "Absolute Champion"?

In November, the NHK Trophy, the sixth of the GP Series, was held in Nagano at the Big Hat which had been the venue for the 1998 Olympics. The SP was scheduled for November 27, and the FS was on the 28th. Chan did not participate in this competition.

■take off 飛び上がる ■entrance 図 入り口 ■classical ballet クラシックバ
レエ ■degree 図 度《角度の単位》 ■pull ~ off 〜をうまくやり通す ■surpass
動〜を上回る

結弦が「血のにじむような努力」を集中させたのは、SPで跳ぶ
２本の４回転だった。１本は「４回転トゥ・ループ＋３回転トゥ・
ループ」の連続ジャンプ。ルールの規定上、プログラムに入れられ
るのは「４回転アクセル」か「難しい助走から跳ぶ４回転」に
なる。アクセルはまだ誰も跳べていないほど難度が高いが、「難
しい助走から跳ぶ４回転」なら手が届く。結弦は、それを「イー
グル」から入る「４回転サルコウ」にしようと考えて猛練習した
のである。「イーグル」は、クラシックバレエで180度に左右に
開く両足のポジションで、両手を鷲（イーグル）のように広げる。
横向きのこの姿勢からステップなしでジャンプ、それも４回転
できる高い跳躍をするのはかなり難しい。だが、結弦には手ご
たえがあった。

得点300点越えで「絶対王者」宣言？

　そして11月、GPシリーズ第６戦のNHK杯が、1998年の五輪
会場だった長野市の「ビッグハット」で開催された。SPは11月
27日、FSは28日。この大会にはチャンは出場しなかったが、３
つ上の無良崇人や同年の田中刑事がライバル的存在だった。日

So Yuzuru's rivals at this event were Takahito Mura, who is three years older than him, and Keiji Tanaka, who is the same age as him. The generation change of the Japanese male skaters was surely happening.

In the SP, Yuzuru's performance was perfect as planned. He cleanly executed a quadruple Salchow entering from an eagle at the beginning. The "quadruple toe loop–triple toe loop" combination and triple axel in the second half of the program were also successful. It was the first time that he had skated without making any mistakes since he changed the program to "Chopin Ballade No. 1." He earned 101.45 points and rewrote his own world record. When he was reviewing his performance after the competition, as he always did, he realized that he wanted to break the record in the FS as well. Once he had honestly admitted the pressure he was under and what he really wanted, he was ready for what lay ahead of him.

On the following day, he performed his FS excellently as well. He landed all the jumps cleanly including three quadruple jumps and two triple axels. His Ina Bauer was beautiful too. Shizuka Arawaka, who was also from Miyagi and the first Japanese female Olympic gold medalist, was very good at the Ina Bauer. So this Ina Bauer was in homage to her, and Yuzuru's flexible body made it

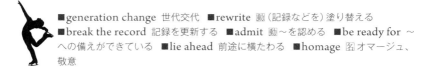

■generation change 世代交代　■rewrite 動（記録などを）塗り替える
■break the record 記録を更新する　■admit 動～を認める　■be ready for ～
への備えができている　■lie ahead 前途に横たわる　■homage 图 オマージュ、
敬意

本男子勢は確実に世代交代の時期に入っていた。

　SPで結弦の演技は作戦通りパーフェクトだった。冒頭のイーグルから入る4回転サルコウ成功、「4回転トゥ・ループ＋3回転トゥ・ループ」の連続ジャンプも成功、後半の3回転アクセルも成功。『バラード第1番』にしてから初めてのノーミスでもあった。得点は101.45。自分の持つ世界記録を更新した。試合後の、いつもの心の整理では、「フリーでも記録を出したい」と思っている自分に気づいた。でも「その欲を認めてしまおう」と思った。いったん、プレッシャーや欲を素直に認めてしまうと前を向ける。

　快進撃は翌日のFSにも続いた。3本の4回転ジャンプと2本の3回転アクセルを含むすべてのジャンプを成功させたのだった。同じ宮城県出身で日本女子初の五輪金メダリストになった先輩・荒川静香が得意とした「イナ・バウワー」も華麗だった。柔軟性のある結弦だからできる彼女へのオマージュでもある。そしてノーミスで演じたFSの得点は216.07。SPと併せた総合得

possible. He performed his FS without any mistakes, and scored 216.07 points. His combined total score was 322.40. He achieved a great record that nobody else before him had ever done. When he saw the score at the Kiss and Cry, he covered his face with his hands. That was the last competition while he was 20 years old.

On the following day, articles with headings such as "Absolute Champion! Yuzuru Hanyu" were printed in many sports papers. In the articles, he was quoted as saying, "I performed while I was telling myself that I'm the 'Absolute Champion.'" But Yuzuru denied this. "On many occasions, I talked a lot. And what I actually said was that I want to become the 'Absolute Champion' at the PyeongChang Olympics. I think my words were misquoted," he said. However, just as Plushenko was called as "Emperor," "Absolute Champion" became Yuzuru's title after that.

But in the sporting world, whether you are a real "Absolute Champion" or not depends on actual records. Not long after the triumph in the NHK Trophy, the GP Final started at the Barcelona International Convention Center in Spain. It was the first time that the GP Final had been held in the same country for two consecutive years. The ISU was trying to revive the popularity of figure skating in Europe. And Spain's Javier Fernandez was regarded as one of the candidates to win this competition. The ISU's intention and Spain's enthusiasm could have been the contributing factors for

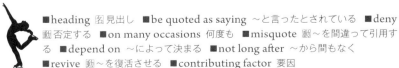

■heading 図 見出し ■be quoted as saying ～と言ったとされている ■deny 動 否定する ■on many occasions 何度も ■misquote 動 ～を間違って引用する ■depend on ～によって決まる ■not long after ～から間もなく ■revive 動 ～を復活させる ■contributing factor 要因

点322.40点。前人未到の大記録を達成した。キス＆クライでその得点を見た結弦は思わず両手で顔を覆った。20歳最後の試合だった。

　翌日、スポーツ新聞などに「絶対王者！ 羽生結弦」の文字が躍った。「自分は『絶対王者』だと言い聞かせながら滑った」ということなのだが、結弦は否定している。「たくさん話した中で、平昌五輪には、『絶対に王者になりたい』といった言葉が独り歩きした」というのが真相のようだ。だが、この「絶対王者」の称号は、あのプルシェンコが「皇帝」との異名で呼ばれるのと同じように、これ以降、結弦の称号になった。

　だが、「絶対王者」の称号にふさわしいかどうかは戦績が決めるのがスポーツの世界である。NHK杯の余韻も冷めやらぬGPファイナルが、スペインの「バルセロナ・インターナショナルコンベンションセンター」で開催された。去年に続いて同じ国でGPファイナルが行なわれるのは初めてのことだが、ヨーロッパでのフィギュア人気復活を図りたいISUと、優勝候補の一人であるハビエル・フェルナンデスの母国スペインの熱意が合致したのだろう。結弦にとっても良い印象の会場だから別に問題はない。それに史上初のGPファイナル3連覇がかかっている。今年

the selection of the venue. As Yuzuru had a good impression about this place, he had no problems with that. He wanted to win the GP Final to be the first in history to achieve a record three-time consecutive win. Yuzuru had just turned 21. The other Japanese male skaters in this event were Daisuke Murakami who is three years older than him, and Shoma Uno who was making his Grand Prix debut at the age of 17.

On December 10, Yuzuru performed the same program perfectly just as he had done at the NHK Trophy. He scored 110.95 and rewrote his personal best. On the 12th, he didn't make any mistakes in the FS either. He earned 219.48 points, which was a better score than Fernandez and Chan in the technical and component elements. His GOE was 3, the maximum points. His combined total was 330.43, more than 40 points ahead of Fernandez who placed second. Yuzuru accomplished a great achievement by beating his own world record for two competitions in a row. He was truly the "Absolute Champion."

Uno, who represents the younger generation after Yuzuru, performed well and came third, and Chan finished in fourth place.

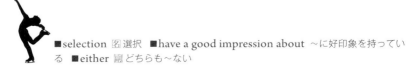

■selection 图 選択　■have a good impression about　～に好印象を持っている　■either 副 どちらも～ない

の日本男子勢は、21歳になった結弦以外は、3つ上の村上大介、ジュニアから上がってきた17歳の宇野昌磨である。

　12月10日のSPはNHK杯と同じ構成でノーミスの完璧な演技。これでまず110.95と自己記録更新。そして12日のFSもノーミス、フェルナンデスやチャンを技術点、構成点でも上回って219.48。出来栄え評価のGOEも上限の3点。総合330.43点で2位のフェルナンデスに40点近く差をつけての圧勝。2戦続けて、自分自身で世界記録を更新するという偉業を達成した。まさに「絶対王者」であった。

　結弦を追う若い世代の日本代表・宇野も3位と健闘、チャンは4位だった。

🎧25 Injuries later in the season

There is a Chinese proverb that "Lights are usually followed by shadows." It means that happy events tend to be accompanied by problems. And this really happened to Yuzuru. He was in top form as the "Absolute Champion" during the first half of the season. After he came back to Japan, he competed at the Japan Championships in December. But he felt pains in his left foot during practice and could hardly be on the ice because of the pain. He endured the pain and won the event anyhow. But he had to take 10 days off after the competition. When he performed in ice shows, he needed to get steroid injections and to take painkillers.

"The inside of my big toe was so painful that I had to shift my ankle to the left when I walked. Because I tried to protect my foot, I couldn't jump at all. I seriously considered withdrawing from the World Championships in March," he said.

After he came back to Toronto, he was treated by a specialist and gradually recovered. But he was told not to do quadruple toe loops. Even if the injuries had healed by the World Championships, there would not have been enough time to practice. He had to lower the program level and try to perform each element perfectly.

■proverb 图 ことわざ　■in top form 絶好調である　■hardly 副 とても～ない　■endure 動 耐える　■anyhow 副 それにも関わらず　■injection 图 注射　■be told not to ～しないように言われる　■even if たとえ～だったとしても

シーズン後半を襲ったケガに苦しむ

　中国から生まれたことわざに「好事魔多し」というのがある。「良いことばかりが続くと悪いことが起こる」という意味で使われるが、シーズン前半を「絶対王者」として絶好調だった結弦が、日本に帰ってから臨んだ12月の全日本選手権では、練習の時から左足に痛みを覚えてリンクに上がれないほどになった。歯をくいしばって耐え、試合では優勝したが、試合後10日間の休み。アイスショーもステロイド注射や痛み止めの薬が必要になった。

　「親指の内側が痛くて、歩く時に足首がアウトサイドの方に行ってしまう。かばって歩くから何も跳べなくなって、3月の世界選手権を棄権するかと悩みました」

　トロントに帰って専門医の治療を受けて少しずつ回復したものの、「4回転トゥ・ループ」禁止令が出た。出場までにケガは回復できたとしても練習が足りなすぎる。プログラム構成の難度を下げて、ひとつずつの完成度を磨く作戦しかなかった。

The World Championships was held at the TD Garden in Boston. Yuzuru had won the silver medal at this event the previous year. He arrived at the TD Garden on March 27. But on the second day of practice, he could not move his body in the way that he wanted. But he had to perform on the 30th. As his condition was so bad, mentally and physically, it looked like it would be impossible for him to perform. But amazingly, his body remembered all the moves which had been building up through long and hard practice sessions. And, to his pleasant surprise, he won. And he made no mistakes! But it was too much for his body after all, and his jumps were not good in the FS on April 1. In the end, his fellow Fernandez won the gold medal, and again, Yuzuru finished in second place.

Although Yuzuru was hurt mentally and physically, he could enjoy the exhibition after the competition. An exhibition is a non-competition show and a traditional event after a figure skating event. Although his moves were limited because of the injury, Yuzuru nicely performed "Requiem of Heaven and Earth" choreographed by Kenji Miyamoto. The music was arranged from the "Requiem for the Great East Japan Earthquake 3.11" by Yasunobu Matsuo. He performed this program with a lot of emotions remembering his feelings and those of the other victims at the time of the disaster.

■look like ～のように思える ■pleasant 形うれしい ■exhibition 名エキシビション ■requiem 名鎮魂歌、レクイエム

前年は銀メダルだった世界選手権はアメリカ・ボストン「TDガーデン」。3月27日に会場入りしたが、練習2日目からは体が動かなかった。その状態で30日のSP本番へ。気持ちも足も「ぐしゃぐしゃで、できるわけない」と思えた。しかし不思議なもので、これまでの長く苦しい練習で積み上げてきたものを身体が覚えていた。なんと1位。それもノーミスで。だが、無理がひびかないわけはなく、4月1日のFSはジャンプが乱れた。同門のフェルナンデスに優勝まで持っていかれ、またも銀メダルに終わった。

　心身ともに傷ついた結弦の心がなごんだのは、試合後のエキシビションだった。勝ち負け抜きで演技を披露するフィギュア界恒例の行事。結弦はできる範囲の動きで、宮本賢二が振付けてくれた『天と地のレクイエム』を丁寧に演じた。松尾泰伸氏作曲の『東日本大震災鎮魂曲「3・11」』をアレンジしたもので、被災した自分や仲間の経験やその時の感情などをたっぷりと込めることができた。

"The disaster was awful, but I'm feeling happy now that I have a chance to skate like this. I'm very thankful to all the people who created this opportunity and who are cheering for me," he said.

In December that year, Yuzuru was featured in a popular Japanese women's magazine "an·an" (published by Magazine House). His picture was on the cover, and a big poster of him was inserted in the magazine. It showed how popular he was. In the interview, he was asked how he felt about having turned 21:

"Nothing has changed, and I want to stay where I am now. Figure skating is not a sport that you can perform in your thirties or forties. So, until then, I'd like to do what I want to do... I'd like to be curious about many things like a child. I'd like to keep on growing and constantly seek to find a way to improve myself. To get better at figure skating technically and artistically, I think that kind of attitude is necessary, and it is very important for me," he explained.

■awful 形恐ろしい　■be featured in ～で特集される　■insert 動 ～を挿入する　■curious 形好奇心の強い　■seek 動探し求める

「被災したけど、こうして滑ることができることの幸せを感じている。その環境を用意し、応援してくれているすべての人への感謝を捧げたい気持ちで一杯になれるんです」

　この年の12月、結弦は日本の人気女性誌『an・an』（マガジンハウス）で特集され、表紙を飾り、折り込みの大きなポスターにもなった。彼の人気ぶりを示している。その中で、21歳になった感想を聞かれてこう答えている。

　「何も変わらないし、このままでいたい。フィギュアは30歳、40歳になっても続けられる競技ではないので、それまでは、ある程度わがままでいたいというか……。子供のようにいろいろなことに好奇心を持ち、向上心を持ち続けて、常に探求心を忘れないでいたい。技術や芸術性を深めるためには、そういう気持ちを持っていなきゃいけないと思うので、そこはすごく大切にしています」

覚えておきたい英語表現

I was thinking too much about not making mistakes. (p. 162, 7行目)
ミスをしないようにと考え過ぎてしまいました。

too は「（〜に加えて）〜も」という意味と、「あまりに〜」という副詞の役割で使います。覚えやすい単語なので、あまり意識して学ぶことが少ないかもしれませんが、話し手・書き手の意図が込められる単語なので、ぜひ多くの使用例を覚えていただきたい単語です。

My wife eats too much.　　　　　私の妻は食べ過ぎる。

This car is too expensive for me.　　この車は僕には高すぎるよ。

too A for B to C という形で「（B にとっては）あまりに A なので C できない」という文法を学校ではよく習いますが、to C の部分がない文をよく見ます。to C が明示されていなくても too A があることで「あまりに A だから…できない」と何かの行動をとることができないことを示唆することに注意しましょう。

This jacket is too small for me.
この上着は僕には小さすぎる。→だから着ることができない

The question was too difficult.
その質問は難しすぎるよ。→だから答えられなかった

もう一つぜひ注意したいのが not 〜 too A「あまり A ではない」という使い方です。

My car was not too expensive.
私の車はそんなに高くありませんでした。（むしろ安かった）

I don't like chocolate too much.
あまりチョコレートは好きじゃない。（チョコレートが嫌いを遠回しに言っている）

「分かりきっている」ように思える単語ほど、調べてみたらたくさんの意味や使い方を持っていることがあります。一つ一つの表現を真摯な姿勢で調べていくことが語彙力アップの秘訣です。

> The disaster was awful. (p. 176, 1行目)
> あの災害はひどかった。

awfulは「とても悪い」「酷い」「不愉快な」という意味の形容詞です。

What an awful smell!　　　なんて酷い臭いだ！

You look awful.　　　（見た目もひどくて）具合が悪そうだよ。

よくないイメージで使われるだけでなく、逆によいイメージで使う場合もあります。

It sounds awful good to me.　それすごくよさそうじゃん。

この場合は副詞として使われています。aweにはもともと「畏れ」「畏敬という意味があり、それがいっぱいに（full）あるという意味でawfulという綴りになっています。
同様のルーツを持つ単語にawesomeもあります。口語で非常によく使われる単語なのでこちらも是非覚えておきましょう。

It's awesome!　　　それすごくいいね！

Awesome!　　　いいね！　美味しいね！　すごい！　etc....

Part 7

The PyeongChang Olympics and beyond

平昌五輪へ、そして未来へ

New program to reveal a different side of Yuzuru

Yuzuru's hobby is to listen to his favorite music. So he is very picky about his earphones and headphones, and he has a big collection of them. Through watching many movies and listening to music a lot, he was able to start suggesting the music for his programs and exhibitions more often. He also became more involved in coming up with ideas for the choreographies and costumes to make them match the theme of the music. "Requiem of Heaven and Earth" and "Seimei" are good examples of his involvement.

For the 2016–2017 season, he could have just continued using the good program from the previous season, but he did not. It seemed that he wanted to expand his possibilities of expression by choosing new programs before the PyeongChang Olympics. His SP music expressed his masculinity and strength, while by contrast his FS music featured his calmness and beauty. The choreographers were the same as in the previous season.

His SP was "Let's Go Crazy" by Prince who died in April that year. His costume was a vest with a marble pattern, pale purple shirt and trousers. Even his shoe covers were purple. It was in homage to Prince who used to wear purple costumes. After the

■picky 形 えり好みがある　■be involved in 〜に関与する　■come up with an idea 案を思いつく　■marble pattern マーブル模様　■pale 形 うすい

新しい結弦が出現する、対照的な構成

　結弦の趣味は、好きな音楽を聴くこと。そのためのイヤホン、ヘッドホンには凝っていてたくさんのコレクションがある。映画を観たり音楽をたくさん聴き込むことで、試合のプログラムやエキシビションで使う曲に、自分から提案することが多くなったし、曲想に合った振付けや衣装にも注文を出すようになった。『SEIMEI』もそうだったし、『天と地のレクイエム』もそうだった。

　2016-2017年は、好評だった前シーズンのプログラムを踏襲して仕上げる選択もあっただろうが、結弦はそうしなかった。韓国・平昌五輪前の1シーズンに、新しい選択をして表現の可能性を広げてみたかったように思える。男っぽさや強さを表すSP曲と、静かさや美しさを表すFS曲での対照的な構成にした。振付師の分担は昨シーズンと同じ。

　SPはこの年4月に亡くなったミュージシャン、プリンスの『Let's Go Crazy』。衣装はマーブル柄のベストに、うすい紫色のシャツとパンツ、靴のカバーまで同色という凝りよう。これは、生前本人が身に着けていた衣装へのオマージュである。荘

solemn sound of the Hammond organ, the sound of a weeping guitar followed, and then it became an up-tempo tune. The erotic yet philosophical lyrics and the choreography synchronized perfectly with each other in this program. It proved that Yuzuru understood this song very deeply.

When it came to the part, "Are we gonna let the elevator bring us down? Oh, no let's go! Go (Go crazy)," Yuzuru did a gesture to represent "crazy" by pointing his index finger to his head in the program. It was as if Yuzuru had become the real Prince and provoked the audience into singing "Come on!" We saw a different side of Yuzuru.

His FS was "Hope and Legacy." It was Yuzuru who gave this title to the program. The original songs were "Asian Dream Song" and "View of Silence" which had been used at the closing ceremony of the 1998 Nagano Paralympics. The music was composed by Joe Hisaishi. The songs were arranged to fit into this new program. The costume was very impressive with a white feather ornament attached to the left shoulder, and a diagonal gradation of white, green and deep blue. His facial expression looked very gentle, and was one that had never been seen on his face before.

Also, he had a new exhibition program, "Notte Stellata (The Starry Night)." It was also known as "The Swan." The music was composed by Saint-Saëns and romantic Italian lyrics had been

■solemn 形荘重な　■weep 動むせび泣く　■philosophical 形哲学的な
■lyric 名歌詞　■index finger ひと差し指　■provoke 動〜を挑発する　■fit
into（長さなどが）合う　■diagonal 形斜めの

重なハモンドオルガンの後、むせぶようなギターがノリの良いアップテンポになる。エロチックさと哲学的な深さを感じる歌詞と振付けがシンクロする。かなり聴き込んでいる証拠だ。

　「下降エレベータで引きずり落とされるままでいいのかい？　やだね、行くぜ！　いっちまえ（いっちまえ）」で、結弦は両ひと差し指を頭に向けて "クレイジー" のジェスチャーをする。プリンスが憑依して観客を「Come on!」と挑発するかのようだ。また違う結弦がそこに現れた。

　FSは『Hope & Legacy』。このタイトルは結弦がつけたものだが、元の曲は、久石譲作曲の「Asian Dream Song（旅立ちの時）」というものと、1998年長野パラリンピック閉会式で使われた「View of Silence」という曲を前後半に合わせて編曲したものだ。左肩に白い羽飾りをつけたコスチュームは、白からグリーン、深い青へのグラデーションが斜めに入った印象的なもの。滑る表情も、今までの結弦にはない柔らかさがあった。

　さらにエキシビションも新しくなった。『ノッテ・ステラータ（星降る夜）』、別名『白鳥』。サン・サーンスの「白鳥」に、イタリア語の歌詞がついた愛を唄うロマンチックな曲だ。振付師は、

added to it. The choreographer was David Wilson who had worked on "Romeo and Juliet" for the Sochi Olympics. Being known as an artistic person, Wilson was expected to be able to reveal Yuruzu's artistic quality.

From "following" to "being followed" by young skaters

During this season, Yuzuru competed using his new programs. The following are his achievements:

In October at Skate Canada, the second GP Series, he placed first in the FS, but failed in the quadruple jumps in the SP. Overall, he finished second behind Chan, trailing by three points.

In November at the NHK Trophy, the sixth GP series, his SP and FS were very good and he won with a score of above 300 points. The second place went to Nathan Chen, a young American skater born in 1999. He had won last year's World Junior Championships, and this event was his debut in a senior-level competition. Keiji Tanaka, who is the same age as Yuzuru, placed third.

In December, the GP Final took place in Marseille. In the FS, Nathan Chen jumped three kinds of quadruples (Lutz, Salchow and toe loop) and placed first. But Yuzuru won overall. It was his fourth straight GP title. Shoma Uno (born in 1997) placed

■add 動 加える　■fail in ～に失敗する　■trail by ~ points ～点差で負けている

ソチ五輪の『ロミオとジュリエット』を手がけたデヴィッド・ウィルソン。芸術家肌のウィルソンが結弦の芸術性を引き出してくれると期待されての起用だ。

「追う立場」から、若手に「追われる立場」へ

　一新したプログラムで臨んだこのシーズンの戦績だけを追っておこう。

　10月のGPシリーズ第2戦スケートカナダ。FSでは勝ったものの、4回転に失敗したSPで負け、チャンに3点差で優勝をさらわれる。

　11月のGPシリーズ第6戦NHK杯。SP、FSとも好調で総合300点超えで優勝。2位は米国の若手（1999年生まれ）のネイサン・チェン。昨年のジュニア王者からの初参戦だった。3位は結弦と同年の田中刑事だった。

　12月のGPファイナルはマルセイユで開催。FSでは、4回転を3種類（4回転ルッツ、4回転サルコウ、4回転トゥ・ループ）も決めたネイサン・チェンに敗れた。だが総合では優勝。これでGPファイナル4連覇になる。3位に入ったのは、日本の若手（1997

third, which was his second consecutive GP title. Yuzuru's rivals Fernandez (fourth) and Chan (fifth) did not perform that great. In contrast, the younger skaters competed very well.

In the same month, Yuzuru withdrew from the Japan Championships because of the flu.

In February 2017, the Four Continents Championships was held at the Gangneung Ice Arena in Gangneung, Korea. It also was a pre-event for the PyeongChang Olympics. Nathan Chen competed in this competition for the first time and won after making five clean quadruple jumps in his FS. Yuzuru competed in this event after a break of four years and won the silver medal. Uno came third.

Up to this point, Yuzuru had been "in the position of chasing" the skaters ahead of him, and had competed with his strong rivals for several years. But now there were many younger skaters, and they could perform quadruple jumps without any problem. The figure skating world was moving into the "quadruple jump era." This competition made him realize that he was now "in the position of being chased." But he was not going to give up the position of "the king" just yet.

■pre-event 图先行イベント　■chase 動〜を追う　■move into 〜に入る
■era 图時代　■just yet とてもまだ（〜しない）

年生まれ）の宇野昌磨、GP 2回連続の3位入賞になった。ライバルの強豪、フェルナンデス（4位）やパトリック・チャン（5位）がやや精彩を欠いたのと対照的な若手の活躍が目立った。

　同月の全日本選手権、結弦は、インフルエンザのために欠場した。

　年が明けた2017年2月、韓国・江陵市の「江陵アイスアリーナ」で開催された四大陸選手権は、平昌五輪のプレイベントでもあった。初出場のネイサン・チェンがFSで5度の4回転ジャンプを成功させて優勝。4年ぶりの出場となった結弦は銀メダル、宇野は3位。

　ずっと先輩たちを「追う立場」であり、強豪たちと競い合ってきた結弦だが、若手がめきめきと台頭し、目の前で軽々と4回転ジャンプを決める「真4回転時代」に入っている。いつしか「追われる立場」に立っていることに気づいた試合だった。しかし、そう簡単に『王者』の座は譲れない。

In March, the World Championships, where "the king would be crowned," was held in Helsinki, Finland. Yuzuru, the two-time consecutive silver medalist in this event, performed poorly and even received deductions. He was fifth in the SP. But he scored a remarkable 223.20 points in the FS, and his combined total score was 321.59. He won the gold medal, for the first time in a long while. Second place went to Uno, and third to Jin Boyang of China. He was born in the same year as Uno (1997), and he was the first skater to cleanly jump four kinds of quadruple jumps in one performance. Also, at this event, many skaters achieved very high scores: Fernandez scored more than 300 (fourth), and Chan (fifth) and Chen (sixth) received more than 290. Some even said that it was "score inflation."

In April, the World Team Trophy was held in Japan. For this event, two men, two women, one figure skating pair and one ice dancing pair with the best results during the season are selected from six countries, and they compete in a team format. Although it is a team event, each athlete still has to fight as an individual. Yuzuru made a mistake on a quadruple jump in the beginning of the SP, which was a "bad habit" of his, and finished seventh. Uno was at the top of the SP scoreboard. But Yuzuru came first in the FS, and led the Japanese team to the gold medal. "I have to apologize to Prince. April 21 is the anniversary of his death, but my performance was miserable," said Yuzuru after the SP on the

■crown 動 栄誉を与える　■first time in a long while 久しぶりに
■inflation 名 暴騰、インフレーション　■apologize to ～に謝る
■anniversary of someone's death（人の）命日

3月は、その『王者』を決める世界選手権がフィンランド・ヘルシンキで開催された。2シーズン連続銀メダルだった結弦は、SPが減点をもらうほどボロボロ（5位）だったものの、FSでは223.20という驚異的な記録を出して総合321.59。久しぶりの金メダルになった。2位は宇野、3位は宇野と同年（1997年生まれ）の中国人、ボーヤン・ジン。ボーヤンこそ2016年に最初に1試合4回転4種のジャンプを成功させた男だ。また、この試合では、4位のフェルナンデスまでが300点超え、5位のチャン、6位のチェンも290点を超えるという極めてレベルの高い内容だった。一部から「点数インフレ」との声も出た。

　4月は、日本で開催された「国別対抗戦」。シーズン上位選手を持つ6ヵ国から男女2人ずつが選出され、個人ではなく参加国の総合順位を競うものである。しかし当然、戦うのは個人である。だが結弦は、SP冒頭4回転ジャンプでミスという"悪い癖"が出て7位になってしまう。SPトップは宇野。FSで逆転して1位になり、団体・日本を金に導いた。結弦は20日のSPの後、「21日がプリンスさんの命日だったのに、不本意な結果で申し訳ないです」と語っていた。全体では、159cmという小さい身体の中に、バネが仕込まれたような宇野の力強い演技が印象的な試合だった。

20th. In this competition overall, Uno's strong performance was very impressive. He moved as if he had a power spring in his small 159 centimeters (five feet two and a half inches) tall figure.

The PyeongChang Olympic season has started

Between May and June in 2017, many ice shows such as "Fantasy on Ice" were held. After a rainy summer, the new season finally started in September. This is the season in which the PyeongChang Olympics will be held—in February, 2018. As usual, the topic at the beginning of the season was program plans. Yuzuru announced his programs. His SP was "Ballade No. 1," and his FS was "Seimei." Some of his fans were surprised because they had thought that Yuzuru would continue to use the song by Prince or "Notte Stellata (The Swan)." But the majority of his fans understood his choice. He had been using "Ballade No. 1" for two seasons since 2014 and had used "Seiei" in the 2015–2016 season. And he was awarded the world's highest scores when he used those programs.

"Using 'Seimei' for the Olympics season is what I've been thinking from the start. As for 'Ballade No. 1', I've performed it many times in the past, and I can be myself when doing it. I don't have to think a lot for those programs. So, that way, I can

■spring 图バネ ■topic 图話題 ■award 動（得点などを）与える ■can be oneself 自然体でいられる

平昌五輪のシーズンが幕を開けた

　2017年5〜6月は、「Fantasy on Ice」（ファンタジー・オン・アイス）などのアイスショーが過ぎ、雨の多かった夏が過ぎ、9月から、いよいよ翌年2月の韓国・平昌五輪を含む新シーズンが始まった。シーズン初めの話題は、例年通り、プログラム・プランのことになる。発表された結弦のものは、SP『バラード第1番』、FS『SEIMEI』だった。これには、プリンスの曲や「白鳥」を続けるものと思っていたファンは驚いたが、「やはり」と納得するファンの方が多かった。『バラード第1番』は2014年から2シーズン続けたもの、『SEIMEI』は2015–2016シーズンで使い、いずれも世界最高得点を生み出したからだ。結弦は説明する。

　「『SEIMEI』は、当初から五輪シーズンで使おうと思っていました。『バラード第1番』は、もう何回も演じてきましたが、自分らしくいられる曲なんです。余計なことを考えなくてすむ。演技の難度をあげることに集中して、自分に勝とうと思います」

concentrate on improving my techniques and I want to push myself harder to get better," he explained.

Yuzuru was thinking about the "quadruple jump era" that was being led by the younger skaters. Nowadays, to win a competition, a skater has to jump four or five quadruples successfully in a performance. Yuzuru had to do it as well. For the quadruple jumps, the toe loop (T), Salchow (S) and loop (Lo) are not good enough. Yuzuru had to execute more difficult jumps such as the flip (F) or Lutz (Lz) consistently. The level of his consecutive combinations of quadruple and triple jumps needed to be extremely high. His strategy, in addition to improving his quadruple jumping techniques, was to try to get more points for the program components score and the GOE about which he had started to feel confident. However, at least four or five skaters could now score a total of 300 points or more.

■push oneself harder 努力する ■good enough 十分である
■extremely 副 極度に

結弦は、若手たちが切り拓いた「真４回転時代」を考えたのだ。
１試合に４回転を４本、５本と取り入れて成功させることが勝利
の方程式になった今、引き下がることはできない。４回転でも
トゥ・ループ（Ｔ）、サルコウ（Ｓ）、ループ（Lo）では通用しない。
難度の高いフリップ（Ｆ）やルッツ（Lz）を安定的に跳ばなければ
ならない。３回転も加えた連続のコンビネーションも異次元のも
のにする。その上で、成熟しつつあると感じている演技構成点
や出来栄え点（ＧＯＥ）の積み上げを狙う作戦になる。何しろ総合
得点で300点を超える選手が４人も５人も出てくるようになった
のだ。

(From here, as readers must have become accustomed to figure skating terms by now, I will use the abbreviations for the types of jumps. Knowing these will be useful when you read or watch news that specializes in figure skating competitions.)

In September, the season started with the 2017 Autumn Classic in Montreal, Canada. On the 22nd in the SP, Yuzuru received 112.72 points to break his own world record. Although the quadruple jump was a S instead of Lo in the second half of the program, it was the first time that he had to execute it cleanly other than at ice shows. The venue was packed with Japanese fans cheering for him with Japanese flags, and it looked as if this competition was being held in Japan. Many thought that Yuzuru's win was almost certain as he was better at the FS than the SP. However, not as many people were aware that Fernandez, one of the other members of "Team Brian," had scored 101.20 just behind Yuzuru.

On the following day, Yuzuru's FS strategy went wrong. He failed on a 3Lz at the opening and could not continue to the next 4Lo. In the latter half of the program, he made a lot of mistakes, and even fell on a 3A, which was usually a very easy one for him. After his performance, he put his hands on his knees and could not move for a while because he was so angry at himself. Because of the pain in his right knee, he reduced the difficulty of his jumps.

■from here ここからは　■be accustomed to 〜に慣れる　■abbreviation 图略語　■specialize in 〜を専門に扱う　■other than 〜以外の　■go wrong 失敗する

（以下、読者も用語に慣れただろうから、ジャンプの種類も略号で書いてみよう。試合の専門的なニュースなどを見る時にも役に立つはずだ。）

　9月からのシーズンの幕開けは、カナダ・モントリオールでの「オータムクラシック2017」だった。22日のSPで、結弦はいきなり自身が持つ世界最高得点を更新する112.72点をマークした。後半の4回転はLoでなくSだったが、ショー以外で決めたのは初めてだった。会場は日本からの大勢のファンで埋まり、日の丸の旗が揺れてまるで国内競技場状態だった。「結弦はSPよりFSが得意だから、優勝に決まったようなもの」という見方が圧倒的だった。歓喜の渦の中で、「ブライアン・チーム」の同僚、フェルナンデスが101.20点ですぐ後ろにつけていることに警戒する人は少なかった。

　翌日、FSで作戦が崩壊した。冒頭の3Lzで失敗、次の4Loができない。後半の、大得意の3Aで転倒するなどミスを連発。演技の後、結弦は悔しさで一杯になり、両膝に手を当てて動けなかった。その右膝の痛みからジャンプの難度を下げたのに失敗したのだ。結局、FSは5位。総合では2位、フェルナンデスが優勝した。

But he failed nonetheless. In the end he placed fifth in the FS, and came second overall. Fernandez was the winner of this event.

But Yuzuru's competitive spirit was still intact. His interview after the event clearly showed this:

"I gained a lot from this competition. Mainly frustration. In my SP, I think the score and my performance has given me a strong sense that I could win at the Olympics. I am competing with myself. I want to push myself further with more difficult programs. I know I have to challenge myself to perform in the way that only I can," he said.

The day "YUZU" becomes a legend

Although this book ends here, I will list his upcoming schedule:

- October 20–22, Cup of Russia, the first event of the GP Series (Moscow)
- November 10–12, NHK Trophy, the fourth event of the GP Series (Osaka)
- December 7–10, GP Final (Nagoya)
  *the 7th is Yuzuru's 23rd birthday
- December 20–24, Japan Championships (Tokyo)

■nonetheless 副 それにも関わらず　■intact 形 損なわれていない
■upcoming 形 今後の

でも、負けん気の結弦は健在だった。試合後のインタビュー
は、いかにも彼らしい。
　「悔しさという大きな収穫を手に入れることができた。SPの
得点や演技内容では『五輪で優勝するぞ』という、自分が強いイ
メージを与えられたと思う。強い自分を追いかけながら、さら
に難しい構成で追い抜いてやろうと思う。やっぱり挑戦しない
と、僕らしい演技は絶対できないと思います」

「YUZU」が伝説のスケーターになる日

　本書は、ここで終わるが、今後のスケジュールだけ紹介して
おこう（変更はあり得る）。
　・10月20 〜 22日、GPシリーズ第1戦　ロシア杯（モスクワ）

　・11月10 〜 12日、同上4戦　NHK杯（大阪）

　・12月7 〜 10日、GPファイナル（名古屋）
　　＊7日は結弦の23歳誕生日
　・12月20 〜 24日、全日本選手権（東京）

In 2018:
- January 22–27, Four Continents Championships (Taipei)
- February 9–25, PyeongChang Olympics (Korea)
  *Unusually, the SP on the 16th and the FS on the 17th start in the morning
- March 19–25, World Championships (Milan)

Since he was in his teens, Yuzuru has been saying, "I will win in the Sochi Olympics, then in PyeongChang as well." But this was not taken seriously at the time. However, he actually made half of it happen in Sochi. I cannot include the results of the PyeongChang Olympics in this book, but I know it will not be an easy one for him. So many skaters nowadays can execute five quadruple jumps in one program and get an overall score of 300 or more. There is even a rumor that the retired "emperor" Plushenko might come back. But whatever the result might be, Yuzuru will keep on fighting. "Figure skating is not the kind of sport you can do when you are in your thirties or forties," Yuzuru has said before. He will still only be 27 at the time of the 2022 Beijing Olympics. I am sure he will fight then as well.

He has often said, "I want to accomplish something that only I can do, and become a legend." Yuzuru is always pushing himself "harder and higher," and he will not change his attitude toward his life. His fans all over the world are fascinated by his way of life, and will continue to cheer him on.

■make ~ happen ～を実現させる ■rumor 图噂 ■cheer ~ on ～に声援を
送る

以下、2018年：
・1月22〜27日、四大陸選手権（台北）
・2月9〜25日、韓国・平昌五輪
　＊SPは16日、FSは17日いずれも異例の午前開始

・3月19〜25日、世界選手権（ミラノ）

　結弦は、10代の頃から「ソチ五輪で優勝して、次の平昌五輪でも優勝します」と公言してきた。当時は本気にされなかったが、まず、その半分は実現して見せた。平昌の結果は本書で追うことはできないが、楽な戦いではないはずだ。「クアドラプル」（4回転）を5本跳ぶ選手、総合得点で300点台を出す選手がひしめいているのだから。一度は引退したはずの「皇帝」プルシェンコ復帰の噂まである。しかし、結果はどうあれ、結弦は戦い続けるだろう。結弦は、「フィギュアは、30歳、40歳になってもやれるスポーツではない」と言っていたが、2022年の北京冬季五輪でもまだ27歳。そこにも挑戦するだろう。

　「世界で唯一無二の、誰もできなかったことをやりとげて、伝説（レジェンド）になりたい」とも言ってきた結弦は、常に「上へ、高みへ」と向かう生き方を変えることはないはずだ。世界に広がった結弦のファンは、その生き方にこそ声援を送り続けるのだ。

覚えておきたい英語表現

I want to push myself harder to get better. (p. 194, 1行目)
もっと上手くなるために、自分をもっと厳しく追い込みたい。

　pushは「〜を押す」という意味の動詞ですが、「人の心」を押す、つまり人に「強く求める」「頑張らせる」という意味もあります。push A to Bで「AにBするよう強く求める」です。

> My parents always pushed me to study.
> 両親はいつも私に学習を強要した。
>
> Don't push yourself too much.
> そんなに無理しないで。
>
> His words pushed me to do something for our city.
> 彼の言葉に触発されて、街のために何かせねばと思った。

　p. 198にも羽生選手が"I want to push myself further,..."（もっと自分を追い込みたい）とpushを使っています。"harder and higher"を追い求め、常に自分に厳しくあろうとする羽生選手の言葉にふさわしい英単語です。

I have to challenge myself to perform in the way that only I can.
(p. 198, 9行目)
僕にしかできないような演技をするために、自分自身に挑戦しないといけないのです。

　羽生選手らしい言葉の中にchallengeという動詞が使われています。多くの日本人にとってとても身近な言葉で、「チャレンジする」という言葉はほぼ日本語として定着していると言ってもいいでしょう。

しかしこのような「カタカナ英語」ほど注意が必要な単語はありません。間違った使い方や意味、ニュアンスが定着していることが多いからです。
　例えばchallengeは"人"を目的語に取る単語で、日本語でよく使われる「(難しい課題など)に挑戦する」という意味はありません。

　　　I challenged Ken to a game of *shogi*.　　ケンに将棋の勝負を挑んだ。

　challengeには「〜に異議を唱える」というとても大事な意味がありますが、これも「カタカナ英語のチャレンジ」にはほとんど含まれないニュアンスですね。

　　　I challenged the judge on his call.　　　審判の判定に異議を唱えた。

challengeは「課題」という意味の名詞で使われることもあります。

　　　That project was a serious challenge for us.
　　　あのプロジェクトは私たちにとって本当に難しい課題だった。

[Appendix] Skating Biography of Yuzuru Hanyu

December 7, 1994	Born in Izumi Ward, Sendai City, Miyagi Prefecture in Japan
1996 (Age 2)	Onset of infantile asthma
1998 (Age 4)	Started skating under the influence of his sister, who was four years older

• 2004–2005 Season (Age 9–10)

October	Japan Novice Championships in the Novice B category	1st
December	Tampere Santa Claus Figure Skating Competition in Finland	1st
*December	Yuzuru's home rink closed due to financial difficulties	

• 2005–2006 Season (Age 10–11)

October	Japan Novice Championships in the Novice B category	2nd

• 2006–2007 Season (Age 11–12)

October	Japan Junior Championships in the Novice A category	3rd
November	Japan Junior Championships	7th
*March	Yuzuru's home rink reopened	

• 2007–2008 Season (Age 12–13)

SP: "Sing, Sing, Sing" (Choreography: Nanami Abe)
FS: "The Firebird" (Choreography: Nanami Abe)
EX: "Amazonic"

October	Japan Junior Championships in the Novice A category	1st
November	Japan Junior Championships	3rd (first time for a novice skater)
March	Copenhagen Trophy	1st

【付録】羽生結弦のスケート年表

1994年12月7日	宮城県仙台市泉区で生まれる
1996年（2歳）	小児喘息を発症
1998年（4歳）	4歳年上の姉の影響でスケートを始める。

●2004–2005シーズン（9–10歳）

10月	全日本ノービス選手権（B）	優勝
12月	フィンランド・サンタクロース杯	優勝
＊12月	ホームリンクが経営難のため閉鎖	

●2005–2006シーズン（10–11歳）

10月	全日本ノービス選手権（B）	2位

●2006–2007シーズン（11–12歳）

10月	全日本ノービス選手権（A）	3位
11月	全日本ジュニア選手権	7位
＊3月	ホームリンク営業再開	

●2007–2008シーズン（12–13歳）

SP 「シング・シング・シング」（振付：阿部奈々美）
FS 「火の鳥」（振付：阿部奈々美）
EX 「アマゾニック」

10月	全日本ノービス選手権（A）	優勝
11月	全日本ジュニア選手権	3位（ノービスの選手では初）
3月	スケート・コペンハーゲン	優勝

• 2008–2009 Season (Age 13–14)

SP: "Bolero" (Choreography: Nanami Abe)
FS: "Rhapsody on a Theme of Paganini" (Choreography: Nanami Abe)
EX: "Change" (By Monkey Majik + Yoshida Brothers)

September	Junior Grand Prix Merano Cup	5th
November	Japan Junior Championships	1st (First win)
December	Debuted at Japan Championships	8th (the youngest participant)
February	All Japan Junior High School Championships	1st
February	World Junior Championships	12th (the youngest participant)

• 2009–2010 Season (Age 14–15)

SP: "Mission Impossible II" (Choreography: Nanami Abe)
FS: "Rhapsody on a Theme of Paganini" (Choreography: Nanami Abe)
EX: "Change" (By Monkey Majik + Yoshida Brothers)

September	Junior Grand Prix Torun Cup	1st (first win)
October	Junior Grand Prix Croatia Cup	1st
November	Japan Junior Championships	1st (two consecutive wins)
December	Junior Grand Prix Final	1st (the record for being the youngest champion)
December	Japan Championships	6th
January	All Japan Junior High School Championships	1st
March	World Junior Championships	1st (the first Japanese junior high student to win)

• 2010–2011 Season (Age 15–16) *Debuted in the senior level

SP: "White Legend" (Choreography: Nanami Abe)
FS: "Zigeunerweisen" (Choreography: Nanami Abe)
EX: "Vertigo" (by U2)

October	GP NHK Trophy	4th

●2008–2009シーズン（13–14歳）

SP「ボレロ」（振付：阿部奈々美）
FS「パガニーニの主題による狂詩曲」（振付：阿部奈々美）
EX「CHANGE」（MONKEY MAJIK＋吉田兄弟）

9月	ジュニアGP メラーノ杯	5位
11月	全日本ジュニア選手権	初優勝
12月	全日本選手権（シニア大会初出場）	8位（出場選手最年少）
2月	全国中学校スケート大会	優勝
2月	世界ジュニア選手権	12位（大会最年少）

●2009–2010シーズン（14–15歳）

SP「ミッション：インポッシブル2」（振付：阿部奈々美）
FS「パガニーニの主題による狂詩曲」（振付：阿部奈々美）
EX「CHANGE」（MONKEY MAJIK＋吉田兄弟）

9月	ジュニアGP トルン杯	初優勝
10月	同上 クロアチア杯	優勝
11月	全日本ジュニア選手権	優勝（2連覇）
12月	ジュニアGP ファイナル	優勝（史上最年少）
12月	全日本選手権	6位
1月	全国中学校スケート大会	優勝
3月	世界ジュニア選手権	優勝（中学生での優勝は日本初）

●2010–2011シーズン（15–16歳）　＊シニアデビュー

SP「ホワイト・レジェンド」（振付：阿部奈々美）
FS「ツィゴイネルワイゼン」（振付：阿部奈々美）
EX「ヴァーティゴ」（U2）

10月	GP NHK杯	4位

November	GP Cup of Russia	7th
December	Japan Championships	4th
February	Four Continents Championships debut	2nd (the record for being the youngest male participant)

● 2011–2012 Season (Age 16–17)

SP: "Étude in D-sharp minor, Op. 8, No. 12" (Choreography: Nanami Abe)
FS: "From a film: Romeo and Juliet" (Choreography: Nanami Abe)
EX: "Somebody to Love" (Justin Bieber)

March	Hit by the Great East Japan Earthquake. Yuzuru's home rink was closed. (Reopened in July.)	
September	Nebelhorn Trophy	1st (first win at a senior-level international competition)
November	GP Cup of China	4th
November	GP Cup of Russia	1st
December	GP Final debut	4th
December	Japan Championships	3rd
March	World Championships debut	3rd (the record for being the youngest Japanese male)

● 2012–2013 Season (Age 17–18)

SP: "Parisienne Walkways" (Choreography: Jeffrey Buttle)
FS: "Notre-Dame de Paris" (Choreography: David Wilson)
EX: "Hello, I Love You" (by The Doors, Choreography: Kurt Browning)
    "Hana Ni Nare" (by Fumiya Sashida, Choreography: Kenji Miyamoto)

October	Finlandia Trophy	1st
October	GP Skate America *a new world record of 95.07 in SP	2nd
November	GP NHK Trophy *beat his own world record with 95.32 in SP	1st
December	GP Final	2nd
December	Japan Championships	1st (first win)

11月	ロシア杯	7位
12月	全日本選手権	4位
2月	四大陸選手権（初出場）	2位（男子選手史上最年少）

●2011–2012シーズン（16–17歳）

SP 「悲愴」（振付：阿部奈々美）
FS 「映画『ロミオ＋ジュリエット』より」（振付：阿部奈々美）
EX 「サムバディ・トゥ・ラブ」（ジャスティン・ビーバー）

3月	東日本大震災に被災、ホームリンクも閉鎖（7月再開）	
9月	ネーベルホルン杯	優勝（シニア国際大会初優勝）
11月	GP 中国杯	4位
11月	GP ロシア杯	優勝
12月	GP ファイナル	4位（初参加）
12月	全日本選手権	3位
3月	世界選手権（初出場）	3位（日本男子史上最年少）

●2012–2013シーズン（17–18歳）

SP 「パリの散歩道」（振付：ジェフリー・バトル）
FS 「ノートルダム・ド・パリ」（振付：デヴィッド・ウィルソン）
EX 「ハロー、アイラブユー」（ドアーズ、振付：カート・ブラウニング）
　　「花になれ」（指田郁也、振付：宮本賢二）

10月	フィンランディア杯	優勝
10月	GP スケートアメリカ ＊SPで世界歴代最高得点（95.07）を記録	2位
11月	GP NHK杯 ＊SPで世界歴代最高得点（95.32）を更新	優勝
12月	GP ファイナル	2位
12月	全日本選手権	初優勝

February	Four Continents Championships	2nd
March	World Championships	4th

● 2013–2014 Season (Age 18–19)

SP: "Parisienne Walkways" (Choreography: Jeffrey Buttle)
FS: "Romeo and Juliet by Nino Rota" (Choreography: David Wilson)

October	Finlandia Trophy	1st
October	GP Skate Canada International	2nd
November	GP Trophée Éric Bompard	2nd
December	GP Final *a new world record of 99.84 in SP	1st (first win)
December	Japan Championships	1st
February	Sochi Olympics	1st
February	Sochi Olympics (team event) *101.45 points in SP	5th
March	World Championships	1st

● 2014 – 2015 Season (Age 19–20)

SP: Chopin "Ballade No. 1" (Choreography: Jeffrey Buttle)
FS: "The Phantom of the Opera" (Choreography: Shae-Lynn Bourne)

November	GP Cup of China	2nd
November	GP NHK Trophy	4th
December	GP Final	1st
December	Japan Championships	1st
March	World Championships	2nd
April	World Team Trophy debut (team event)	1st

● 2015–2016 Season (Age 20–21)

SP: Chopin "Ballade No. 1" (Choreography: Jeffrey Buttle)
FS: "Seimei" (Choreography: Shae-Lynn Bourne)
EX: "Requiem of Heaven and Earth" (Choreography: Kenji Miyamoto)

October	GP Skate Canada International	2nd
November	GP NHK Trophy *beat the world record with a combined total score of 322.40	1st

2月	四大陸選手権	2位
3月	世界選手権	4位

●2013–2014シーズン（18–19歳）

SP 「パリの散歩道」（振付：ジェフリー・バトル）
FS 「ニノ・ロータ 映画『ロミオとジュリエット』より」
　　（振付：デヴィッド・ウィルソン）

10月	フィンランディア杯	優勝
10月	GP スケートカナダ	2位
11月	GP エリック・ボンパール（フランス）杯	2位
12月	GPファイナル ＊SPで世界歴代最高得点（99.84）を記録	初優勝
12月	全日本選手権	優勝
2月	ソチ五輪（個人戦）	優勝（金）
2月	ソチ五輪（団体戦） ＊SPで101.45点	5位
3月	世界選手権	優勝

●2014–2015シーズン（19–20歳）

SP ショパン「バラード第1番」（振付：ジェフリー・バトル）
FS 「オペラ座の怪人」（振付：シェイ＝リーン・ボーン）

11月	GP 中国杯	2位
11月	GP NHK杯	4位
12月	GPファイナル	優勝
12月	全日本選手権	優勝
3月	世界選手権	2位
4月	国別対抗戦（初出場）	1位

●2015–2016シーズン（20–21歳）

SP ショパン「バラード第1番」（振付：ジェフリー・バトル）
FS 「SEIMEI」（振付：シェイ＝リーン・ボーン）
EX 「天と地のレクイエム」（振付：宮本賢二）

10月	GP スケートカナダ	2位
11月	GP NHK杯 ＊合計点が322.40の世界記録	優勝

December	GP Final *retained his own world record with a combined total score of 330.43	1st
December	Japan Championships	1st
March	World Championships	2nd

● 2016–2017 Season (Age 21–22)

SP: "Let's Go Crazy" (Choreography: Jeffrey Buttle)
FS: "Hope and Legacy" (Choreography: Shae-Lynn Bourne)
EX: "Notte Stellata" (Choreography: David Wilson)

October	GP Skate Canada International	2nd
November	GP NHK Trophy	1st
December	GP Final	1st
February	Four Continents Championships	2nd
March	World Championships *scored 223.30 in FS	1st
April	World Team Trophy (team event)	

● 2017–2018 Season (Age 22–23)

SP: Chopin "Ballade No. 1" (Choreography: Jeffrey Buttle)
FS: "Seimei" (Choreography: Shae-Lynn Bourne)

September	Skate Canada Autumn Classic International *received 112.72 points in the SP; beat his own world's highest score	2nd
October	GP Cup of Russia	2nd
November	GP NHK Trophy	Withdrew

(The following schedule is to be confirmed)

December	Japan Championships	
January	Four Continents Championships	
February	PyeongChang Olympics	
March	World Championships	

12月	GPファイナル ＊合計330.43で世界最高得点を更新	優勝
12月	全日本選手権	優勝
3月	世界選手権	2位

●2016−2017シーズン（21−22歳）

SP 「Let's Go Crazy」（振付：ジェフリー・バトル）
FS 「Hope & Legacy」（振付：シェイ゠リーン・ボーン）
EX 「ノッテ・ステラータ」（振付：デヴィッド・ウィルソン）

10月	GPスケートカナダ	2位
11月	GP NHK杯	優勝
12月	GPファイナル	優勝
2月	四大陸選手権	2位
3月	世界選手権 ＊FSで223.20得点	優勝
4月	国別対抗戦	

●2017−2018シーズン（22−23歳）

SP ショパン「バラード第1番」（振付：ジェフリー・バトル）
FS 「SEIMEI」（振付：シェイ゠リーン・ボーン）

9月	カナダ オータムクラシック ＊SPで112.72点、世界最高得点を更新	2位
10月	GP ロシア杯	2位
11月	GP NHK杯	欠場

（以下、未定）

12月	全日本選手権	
1月	四大陸選手権	
2月	韓国・平昌五輪	
3月	世界選手権	

【参考資料】

・『羽生結弦 王者のメソッド 2008-2009』(野口美穂著 文芸春秋刊)

・『蒼い炎』(羽生結弦 扶桑社刊)

・『蒼い炎 Ⅱ』(羽生結弦 扶桑社刊)

・『羽生結弦語録』(羽生結弦 ぴあ刊)

・雑誌『an・an』2015.12.16号(マガジンハウス刊)

・公益財団法人 日本スケート連盟

　ホームページ　http://skatingjapan.or.jp/

・株式会社ジェイ・スポーツ(Jsports)

　ホームページ　https://www.jsports.co.jp/skate/

English **C**onversational **A**bility **T**est
国際英語会話能力検定

● E-CATとは…
英語が話せるようになるための
テストです。インターネット
ベースで、30分であなたの発
話力をチェックします。

www.ecatexam.com

● iTEP®とは…
世界各国の企業、政府機関、アメリカの大学
300校以上が、英語能力判定テストとして採用。
オンラインによる90分のテストで文法、リー
ディング、リスニング、ライティング、スピー
キングの5技能をスコア化。iTEP®は、留学、就
職、海外赴任などに必要な、世界に通用する英
語力を総合的に評価する画期的なテストです。

www.itepexamjapan.com

[IBC対訳ライブラリー]
英語で読む羽生結弦

2018年1月11日　第1刷発行

著　者　土屋晴仁

訳　者　佐藤和枝

発行者　浦　晋亮

発行所　IBCパブリッシング株式会社
　　　　〒162-0804 東京都新宿区中里町29番3号 菱秀神楽坂ビル9F
　　　　Tel. 03-3513-4511　Fax. 03-3513-4512
　　　　www.ibcpub.co.jp

印刷所　中央精版印刷株式会社
CDプレス　株式会社ケーエヌコーポレーションジャパン

ISBN978-4-7946-0519-1